Suffocating Stagnation

Ignite Momentum for Peak Performance

STEPHANIE CUNHA, Ph.D.

DISCLAIMER
All information presented in this book is for educational and resource purposes only. It is not a substitute for, or a supplement to, any advice given to you by your physician or healthcare provider. You are solely responsible for how information is perceived and utilized, and you apply the concepts in this book at your own risk. No persons associated with Mental Accelerator will be held responsible for any injuries or problems that may occur due to the use of this book or the advice contained within.

COPYRIGHT NOTICE
Published by Mental Accelerator
Portland, Oregon
www.mentalaccelerator.com
Copyright ©2025 by Mental Accelerator
All rights reserved.

Cover design by Stephanie Cunha
Illustrations: Max Uak, copyright ©2025 Mental Accelerator

Library of Congress Control Number: 2024921244
Print ISBN: 978-1-960424-03-7
eBook ISBN: 978-1-960424-04-4

No part of this book may be used or reproduced without written permission from the copyright holder.

Printed in the United States of America on acid-free paper.
First Edition

True happiness comes from the joy of deeds well done, the zest of creating things new.
　—Antoine de Saint-Exupéry.

CONTENT

CONTENT 3

Introduction 1

SECTION 1 Overcoming Inertia 9

Forward Motion Necessity 9

Stagnation Trap 13

The Cycle of Sameness 16

Catalyst for Change 18

Overcoming Resistance 21

Closing Open Loops 26

SECTION 2 Artificially Creating Momentum 33

Momentum Perception 34

Rehearsing Momentum 38

Crafting Excitement 40

Feedback Loop Design 43

Get to Work 46

Your Next Strategic Move 48

The Power of Basics 53

SECTION 3 Priming Momentum 59

Morning Momentum 60

History Repeats Itself 65

Create habit loops 68

Motion Creates Momentum 71

Quantum Leap Days 74

The Bugenhagen Method 78

SECTION 4 Steering Momentum 83

The First Law of Physics 84

Purpose-Driven 88

Scenario Analysis 90

Backward Momentum 93

Course Correction 96

Momentum Mapping 100

SECTION 5 Seizing Opportunities 105

Embrace the side quest. 105

Ready for the Unexpected 110

Making Timely Decisions 115

The Rhythm of Success 117

Impulsive Action 127

SECTION 6 Sustaining Momentum............ 133

Plan for Periodic Resets 133

Seeking Adventure 136

Gain Perspective 141

Implement a challenge day. 147

Harnessing Physical Motion 150

Conclusion... 153

INTRODUCTION

There are moments when we all feel trapped, as if suffocating under the weight of monotony and stagnation. You're hungry for more and gasping for air. You look around and realize each day is a carbon copy of the last. There's no growth, no progress, no forward movement. You're stuck in a loop of sameness.

I've experienced this suffocation twice, and both times, it felt unbearable. I was utterly drained of motivation and drive because it seemed like nothing I did made a difference. The harder I worked, the more it felt like I was sinking into a quicksand of inactivity. There were no results, no feedback, nothing indicating that all my efforts were bearing any fruit. And in those moments, the suffocation felt all too real.

The natural response to challenges is often trying harder and putting in more effort. While this mindset dwells in determination and resilience, it frequently leads to burnout and frustration.

It's an interesting paradox. You're working so hard because you want to present the best version of yourself to the world and make strides toward your goals.

But...

> "More effort alone is rarely the answer."

When you're trapped in that cycle, it's easy to feel hopeless. It feels as if your efforts don't matter. It's discouraging. When that feeling sets in, and you stop believing that your actions have any meaningful impact—it drains the life out of you. You start questioning why you're doing what you're doing in the first place. Why keep trying when nothing seems to change?

The first time I experienced this kind of suffocation, it hit me hard. I had dreams, ambitions, and a clear vision for my future. But every single day felt like a battle against the weight of repetition. I would wake up, go through the motions, and face the same routine, obstacles, and lack of fulfillment. I wanted to shake things up, but I didn't know how. I didn't know where to start.

When you're caught in the grip of stagnation, it's not just a matter of feeling trapped—it's also about the helplessness that comes with not knowing how to escape it. You start doubting yourself. Maybe it's you. Perhaps you're not working hard enough or smart enough.

The absence of momentum leaves you running in place, stuck in a rut with no progress in sight.

Imagine being trapped in quicksand, with each attempt to break free only sinking you more profoundly into stagnation. It's frustrating and disheartening to feel like the world is moving on while you remain stuck, unable to break free from the inertia holding you back.

This feeling of inertia intensifies when you watch family and friends thriving, chasing their dreams, and making significant strides in their lives. Each success they achieve is a sharp reminder of your lack of progress, deepening the sense of isolation.

You find yourself grappling with inadequacy, questioning why you can't seem to evolve or find direction. The weight of this comparison is heavy, leading to a cycle of self-doubt and frustration. While they celebrate milestones, you are a spectator sidelined in a race you desperately want to join.

This experience is a relentless tug-of-war between aspiration and reality, where your inner drive clashes with the reality of your situation. You may yearn for a breakthrough, a sign that movement is possible, yet each day seems to blend into the next, leaving you feeling more lost than before. The frustration stems from your current state and the awareness that change is possible and that others are making the strides you desire.

We're not meant to live in a state of stagnation. We're meant to grow, evolve, and thrive. And when we're not, our bodies, minds, and spirits rebel, resulting in a suffocating feeling.

For me, recognizing that was the first step in breaking free. It wasn't easy, and it didn't happen overnight. The second time I experienced this stagnation, pulling myself out of it was even more difficult. I'd been through it once before, and I thought I'd learned how to avoid it. Growth isn't linear. There are setbacks. There are plateaus. And sometimes, there are moments when it feels like all the progress you've made is slipping away.

That feeling of suffocation is a sign. It highlights recognizing your potential and the steps to move beyond the sidelines. It's a signal from your deeper self, telling you it's time for a change. It's not a condemnation of your efforts but a reminder that something needs to shift.

Suffocation is not a sign of failure. It is an opportunity for transformation. When we're too comfortable, we don't grow. When we're pushed to our limits, feeling trapped and desperate for more, actual growth begins.

The suffocation you feel in those moments is a signal. It's telling you it's time to make a change. Instead of pushing harder, realize that more effort alone isn't the answer. What you need is momentum. Shifting your focus to ignite momentum brings the air back, helping you breathe freely again. You start moving step by step toward the life you're meant to live, even if they're small steps.

The real secret is in building momentum, not just exerting effort. Every step you take is amplified when your actions are fueled by momentum, leading to growth and meaningful progress. Unlike pure effort, which can feel like an uphill battle, momentum creates a compounding effect, turning small actions into powerful achievements.

> "In every scenario, momentum matters more than effort."

Effort, while essential for starting, has a limited capacity. When considering effort, it should always be within the context of momentum.

Ask yourself: will this multiply or neutralize my effort? This shift in perspective will change how you approach challenges and opportunities.

Conversely, when you struggle against the tide, your energy dissipates without significant advancement. Understanding this dynamic is key.

Imagine riding a bicycle. At the start, pedaling is tough, and you exert considerable effort to gain speed. But once you reach a certain velocity, the bike moves with minimal additional effort. This is momentum in action. Seeking momentum means finding ways to sustain and build upon your current speed rather than constantly straining to pedal harder.

The effort is the immediate energy you spend on a task. It encompasses the long hours, the grit, and your relentless push against obstacles. While effort is essential, it is finite; it has its physical and mental limits. Pushing yourself harder might yield short-term gains, but it's not a sustainable strategy for long-term success.

To achieve lasting success, stop thinking about trying harder. Instead, focus on building and sustaining momentum.

By shifting your perspective and aligning your efforts with momentum, you'll find your efforts are not only more effective but more enjoyable. The path to your goals will become a journey of increasing ease and speed, driven by the powerful force of momentum.

Looking back on those two periods of stagnation, I now see them as blessings. They were painful, yes. They were frustrating and, at times, deeply disheartening. But they forced me to dig deep and find the strength to keep going. They revealed that I'm capable of more than I ever imagined. Most importantly, they reminded me that no matter how trapped or suffocated I may feel in the moment, there's always a way out. There's always a way forward.

If you're feeling that suffocation right now, know you're not alone. Know that it's not a sign of failure or weakness. It's a sign that you're ready for something more. You're ready to break free from the cycle of sameness and step into a new chapter of growth, possibility, and fulfillment. The air you're craving awaits you to take that first breath.

SECTION 1 OVERCOMING INERTIA

The hardest part of creating momentum is taking the first step. It's that initial push—when you summon the courage and conviction to break free from inertia and set your intentions into motion. But taking that first step isn't easy. It requires courage, determination, and a willingness to embrace the unknown. You must confront your fear of failure, rejection, and uncertainty and push past them with unwavering resolve. It's a leap of faith, a leap into the unknown, with no guarantee of success.

FORWARD MOTION NECESSITY

*****

> To grasp momentum's importance, you must recognize its necessity. To feel content, fulfilled, and truly alive, you must move forward consistently. The absence of progress leads to malaise, where life feels like it is slipping away from you.

In my work with athletes, feeling stuck is a common lament. They often describe their lives as being on pause, their dreams deferred, or their potential unrealized.

John is a prodigious runner with Olympic dreams. John's journey was marked by the highs of early success and the crushing lows of injuries that struck just as he was gaining momentum. A torn Achilles tendon followed by a fractured ankle left him trapped in a relentless cycle of recovery and reinjury. Each setback was not merely a physical hurdle but a blow to his spirit, eroding his confidence and dampening his once unshakable determination.

Despite his unwavering dedication to grueling physical therapy sessions and relentless training regimens, John felt he was running in place, unable to catch up to his peers, who continued to excel. The stagnation was suffocating, casting a shadow over his once-bright aspirations and making him question if he would ever reclaim his former glory on the track.

> In this sense, Momentum is not just a physical principle but a psychological necessity.

Human beings are inherently goal-oriented creatures. You derive a sense of purpose and satisfaction from setting and achieving goals, whether small daily tasks or significant life ambitions.

From the ancient civilizations of Mesopotamia and Egypt to the Greek and Roman empires, historical records abound with evidence of humanity's goal-oriented nature. Whether building monumental structures like the Great Pyramids or conquering vast territories, your ancestors were driven to leave their mark on the world to accomplish something enduring.

It's not just about setting goals; it's about striving for mastery.

> Proficiency makes momentum compound like so: the better you get at something, the more appealing it is. As you become more adept in your endeavors, your confidence grows, and your passion intensifies.

True happiness comes from the joy of deeds well done, the zest of creating things new.
—Antoine de Saint-Exupéry.

Proficiency is an endless source of satisfaction. Take, for example, an athlete who dedicates countless hours to perfecting their craft. Each improvement brings a surge of momentum, driving them to push harder and reach new achievements.

In this way, proficiency is a catalyst, propelling you to success and fulfillment.

> Making progress, no matter how incremental, reinforces your sense of competence and efficacy. It confirms that you can influence your circumstances and steer your life in the desired direction.

This forward motion is essential for your mental and emotional health. Research in psychology has shown that progress, even in small doses, triggers the release of dopamine, the brain's reward chemical. This not only makes you feel good but motivates you to continue striving.

> It's a positive feedback loop: progress fuels motivation, and motivation fuels further progress.

A positive feedback loop is essential for fostering progress and motivation. When you get wins, it fuels your desire to keep moving forward. This cycle creates momentum, making it easier to tackle new challenges.

While failure is essential for learning, too much of it without any positive outcomes can sap your motivation. It's crucial to balance setbacks with tangible successes that build your confidence. Celebrating wins reinforces the idea that progress is achievable, providing a counterweight to the discouragement of failure.

Even though you naturally want to move forward, you often encounter a formidable obstacle: stagnation.

STAGNATION TRAP

*****

Stagnation is like being trapped in quicksand; the harder you struggle to break free, the deeper you sink. Every attempt to make progress feels futile, leaving you in a state of inertia where change seems impossible despite your best efforts and intentions.

> It is frustrating to feel stuck as if you're on the sidelines of your life while everything around you moves forward.

The roots of stagnation can stem from various sources. One common cause is fear—fear of failure, fear of the unknown, or fear of stepping outside your comfort zone. This apprehension paralyzes you, making you hesitate to take action even when you know you need to. Another source can be negative self-talk, where doubt and criticism drown out your inner voice of encouragement. When you keep telling yourself that you're incapable or will never succeed, finding the motivation to try becomes harder.

External factors also play a significant role in stagnation. Life's responsibilities, work, family obligations, and financial pressures can weigh heavily on you, leaving little room for personal growth or exploration. In some cases, the environments, whether toxic workplaces or unsupportive relationships, can stifle your ability to move forward and explore new opportunities.

A lack of clear goals can contribute to stagnation. Without a defined direction, it's easy to feel adrift, unsure of what steps to take next. Even if you desire to make a change, the absence of a roadmap is overwhelming. You don't know where to focus your energy without specific goals to guide you. This uncertainty drains your motivation, making it harder to take action.

You might feel stuck in a cycle of wanting to improve but not knowing how to start.

Recognizing the sources of stagnation is the first step toward breaking free. Addressing these underlying issues, whether reframing your mindset, seeking support, or setting clear, actionable goals, can help you regain momentum.

Imagine yourself as an aspiring athlete, dreaming of reaching the top of your sport. You spend countless hours training, giving everything you have, only to be sidelined by injury after injury. Each setback chips away at your progress and confidence, leaving you feeling stuck. Your dreams of competing at the highest level seem further out of reach, and the future you once envisioned feels distant.

As you cope with the physical and emotional toll of your injuries, time feels like it's standing still, and uncertainty clouds your way forward.

Imagine you're working hard to master a new skill, pouring in effort but never quite getting it right. Each attempt frustrates you, and you wonder if success is possible. Then, as you watch others nail the move with what looks like zero effort, that feeling of being stuck only grows stronger, leaving you caught in a loop of self-doubt and stagnation.

In both cases, you face the tough challenge of breaking free from stagnation and finding a way to reignite your progress.

> Whether it's a slump in performance, a plateau in skill development, or exhaustion from relentless training, the common thread in stagnation is a perceived lack of progress.

Stagnation is detrimental.

When you feel stuck, it often leads to frustration, anxiety, and even depression. As an athlete trapped in stagnation, this becomes a breeding ground for a whirlwind of negative emotions. Frustration bubbles up as you struggle with the invisible constraints holding you back. Anxiety eats away at your inner peace, constantly reminding you of the uncertain future that looms ahead.

THE CYCLE OF SAMENESS

*****

The cycle of sameness is a phenomenon where each day blends seamlessly into the next, devoid of any meaningful variation or progress.

It's a monotonous loop of routines and activities lacking excitement, leaving you trapped in a perpetual state of inertia.

> Each day feels like a replay of the one before—a relentless loop of wake, work, eat, sleep, repeat. Activities that once felt exciting have faded into a routine, now just empty repetitions with no spark or freshness.

It's a suffocating existence where the weight of routine snuffs out even the slightest glimmer of spontaneity. What once held promise and excitement has become mundane and uninspiring, leaving you stranded in an endless desert of stagnation.

Those caught in the cycle of sameness often describe their experiences vividly, expressing frustration and disillusionment with their lives' repetitive nature. They yearn for change and advancement yet find themselves unable to break free from the relentless grip of routine.

This cycle is not merely about physical inactivity; it represents a more profound, existential form of stagnation, where life feels stagnant and devoid of purpose.

> When you're in stagnation, even the slightest setback can feel monumental. Without forward momentum, there's no progress to counterbalance these small losses, so each misstep looms more significant than it otherwise would.

In these moments, setbacks are like evidence confirming your worst fears—that things aren't moving or, worse, are sliding backward. This perception deepens the cycle of stagnation, creating a mindset where every small mistake or delay seems catastrophic, eroding confidence and reinforcing self-doubt. Without forward movement, there's no "win" to counterbalance these moments, no small victory to remind you that progress is still within reach.

Without a sense of forward motion or progress, you may find yourself stuck in a cycle of sameness, struggling to find meaning and fulfillment in your life. As time slips away, it feels like you're missing out on notable achievements or milestones that could mark your journey.

CATALYST FOR CHANGE

*****

For some, the catalyst for change arrives unexpectedly, much like a sudden injury sidelining an athlete during their peak season. A star athlete who has been training tirelessly for an upcoming championship suffers a devastating injury that abruptly halts their progress.

This unforeseen event disrupts their physical routine, challenges their mental resilience, and forces them to reevaluate their priorities.

An external event—a job loss, a new opportunity, or a significant life change—that shakes you out of your comfort zone and thrusts you into the unknown often becomes your catalyst for change.

> These external shocks serve as wake-up calls, breaking the illusion of stability and forcing you to face your reality directly.
>
> The solid ground you once relied on suddenly turns uncertain, leaving you disoriented and exposed.

As the athlete grapples with their injury, they confront their body's limitations and their career's fragility. They must navigate the emotional rollercoaster of disappointment, frustration, and uncertainty as they come to their new reality.

Yet, within this adversity lies the potential for growth and transformation. The athlete learns to adapt to their circumstances, exploring new avenues for rehabilitation and discovering inner reservoirs of strength and resilience they never knew they possessed.

Similarly, unexpected setbacks serve as powerful catalysts for change. Losing a job can push you toward a new career path. A breakup may spark self-reflection and growth. A health scare can inspire you to focus on your well-being. These unexpected challenges often lead to a brighter future.

> When faced with uncertainty, life offers you a chance to reevaluate your goals, reassess your priorities, and realign your actions with your true aspirations. It's an opportunity to break free from complacency and embrace the unknown with courage and determination.

While the journey may be fraught with challenges and obstacles, you will also find growth, transformation, and fulfillment opportunities.

For others, the catalyst for change must be self-initiated—a conscious decision to break free from stagnation and carve out a new path forward.

This self-initiated catalyst requires courage and determination. It entails stepping out of your comfort zone and embracing new experiences and perspectives. It demands that you dream beyond your current circumstances and take bold leaps of faith into the unknown.

> Regardless of how the catalyst for change manifests, its purpose remains: to shake you from complacency and propel you to a brighter future.

It acts as a beacon of light in the darkness, guiding you to new horizons and opportunities for growth. It serves as a reminder that life is too short to remain stagnant, urging you to reassess your priorities, reevaluate your goals, and realign your actions with your deepest aspirations.

The catalyst for change ignites the spark of transformation within you, setting a fire of determination and resilience ablaze. It challenges you to rise above adversity, embracing the journey of self-discovery and personal growth. It reminds you that even in uncertainty, you can shape your destiny and create your desired life.

So, whether the catalyst for change comes from within or is external, let it be the catalyst that propels you to a brighter, more fulfilling future.

OVERCOMING RESISTANCE

*****

What holds you back from taking that first step?

Often, it's resistance—the voice of doubt and self-criticism whispering in your ears, telling you you're not good enough, not ready enough, or not deserving enough.

It's the fear of failure, the fear of judgment, and the fear of stepping outside your comfort zone and into the unknown.

But here's the truth: resistance and fear are natural parts of the process. They're the guardians of your comfort zone, the gatekeepers of the status quo, and if you want to create momentum in your life, you must learn to confront and overcome them.

In martial arts, a skilled practitioner learns to overcome resistance and inertia. They adapt to their opponent's movements and use their energy to their advantage.

> Pursuing your goals will require resistance, internal doubts, external challenges, and moments of stagnation.
>
> Overcoming these obstacles and redirecting their energy is critical to igniting momentum.

Trusting in the Process

Whenever you learn a skill, you frequently reach a point of frustration; what you are learning seems beyond your capabilities.

When you give in to these feelings, you unconsciously quit on yourself before you give up. The difference is not simply a matter of determination but trust and faith.

> Many people who succeed in life have the experience of mastering a skill in their youth—whether it's a sport, a musical instrument, a language, or something else. Embedded in their minds is the feeling of pushing past frustration and reaching that cycle of rapid improvement. In moments of doubt, these memories resurface, reminding them to trust the process. With this confidence, they keep going long after others have slowed down or mentally given up.

Mastering a skill relies on time as the magic ingredient; with consistent practice day after day, parts of the skill start to feel natural and ingrained. Gradually, you internalize the entire skill; it becomes a part of your nervous system. Your mind transcends the minutiae and perceives the broader picture. This miraculous sensation is within reach through practice, regardless of your inherent talent level.

The primary impediments to this progress are your emotions, boredom, panic, frustration, and insecurity. These emotions are expected, and everyone experiences them. You cannot suppress them but manage them with faith in the process.

> Boredom fades once you fully engage in the cycle."

> Panic subsides after repeated exposure. Frustration signals progress. It shows that your mind is grappling with complexity and needs more practice. Insecurities will transform into confidence as you gain mastery.

By trusting this will happen, you allow the natural learning process to fall into place. Overcoming resistance and fear lies in trusting the process. It involves believing in yourself and your ability to navigate the challenges ahead. It's about recognizing that growth and progress often come with discomfort and uncertainty—and embracing the journey, imperfections and all.

Taking that first step is not about having all the answers or knowing exactly how things will unfold. It's about trusting that each step, no matter how small it may seem, brings you closer to your goals. It's about having faith in the power of momentum. Once you set the wheels in motion, progress will naturally follow.

Starting Small: The Power of Incremental Progress

Starting small is incredibly powerful when taking the first step. Rather than tackling your goals all at once, break them into smaller, more manageable tasks and focus on making incremental progress each day.

Consider an athlete learning a new skill, such as a tennis player mastering their backhand. Instead of attempting to perfect the entire motion in one go, they might start by focusing on one aspect, such as their grip or footwork. They practice and refine each individually by breaking down the skill into smaller components, gradually building their proficiency over time. This approach allows them to make steady progress without feeling overwhelmed by the complexity of the task.

Celebrating Every Victory

As you take those first tentative steps toward your goals, it's important to celebrate every victory along the way, no matter how small. Whether it's completing a task on your to-do list, overcoming a fear or obstacle, or simply showing up and putting in the work, each victory is a testament to your progress and resilience.

Celebrating these victories boosts your morale and motivation and reinforces the positive feedback loop of momentum. It's a reminder that you're making progress and moving in the right direction, and with each step, you're inching closer to your ultimate goals.

CLOSING OPEN LOOPS

*****

Trusting the process entails taking small, consistent steps and celebrating each victory. But where does one begin?

One potent strategy for kick-starting momentum in life involves addressing what we refer to as "open loops."

This concept emerged from observations of clients grappling with many challenges, often attempting multiple mindset strategies simultaneously before a competition. They'd embark on one approach only to abandon it for another without seeing it through. Despite their enthusiasm and potential in these discussions, they frequently failed to translate into tangible actions. The outcome? A slew of open loops, tasks, and ideas started but left incomplete.

An open loop is anything in your life that requires closure, such as unfinished tasks, unfulfilled goals, and uncompleted projects. These things occupy mental space and drain your energy, creating a sense of unease and hindering your ability to move forward.

The nature of existence is such that things only have power when you finish and complete them in full. Anything that's only partially completed carries zero percent of its potential value.

Partial progress without completion feels like no progress at all.

Consider a student working on their thesis. Imagine they've written 90% of their research paper but leave the last section unwritten. Despite the substantial progress, that last 10% is crucial.

They can't submit their thesis, earn their degree, or advance their academic and professional career without completing it. All the effort they put into the first 90% is useless until they fully complete the project.

This example shows that even near completion doesn't yield results, highlighting the importance of closing open loops to harness the benefits of your efforts and move forward effectively.

> The journey to initiating and sustaining momentum in life is intricately linked to your ability to close open loops. Systematically addressing these unfinished tasks and projects creates a foundation for continuous progress and personal growth.
>
> This process enhances your productivity and enriches your mental and emotional well-being.

The impact of open loops on your life is profound. Each unresolved task or unfinished project creates mental drag, a constant background noise that disrupts your focus and productivity.

As the number of open loops accumulates, so does the feeling of being trapped in a cycle of sameness, where each day blends into the next without meaningful progress or growth.

In this way, open loops become insidious barriers to change, perpetuating a state of stasis that stifles your potential and dims the light of possibility.

Thus, recognizing and addressing open loops is essential to breaking free from stagnation and reigniting the spark of momentum in your life.

> One effective strategy for harnessing the power of momentum is keeping a comprehensive log of all your open loops and resolving to close them from the easiest to the hardest.

This method has multiple benefits:

- Closing small loops provides immediate satisfaction and a sense of accomplishment, boosting your motivation to tackle more complex tasks.
- Completing tasks, even minor ones, builds confidence and reinforces your ability to achieve goals. Each closed loop is a testament to your capability and discipline.
- Reducing the number of open loops clears mental space, allowing you to focus more effectively on significant projects without the constant distraction of unfinished business.

Practical Steps to Close Open Loops

1) Create an open loop log. Start by writing down all your open loops, from minor errands to significant projects. Be thorough and honest—capture every task that requires closure.

2) Prioritize and plan. Organize the loops from the easiest to the hardest. This prioritization helps you gain quick wins, creating a positive momentum that carries you forward.

3) Allocate time. Dedicate specific time blocks to closing these loops. Consistency is key—make it a part of your daily or weekly routine to address these tasks systematically.

4) Eliminate unnecessary loops. You may not need to close all your loops. Some tasks may no longer be relevant or necessary. Identify these and remove them from your list, reducing unnecessary mental burden.

5) Celebrate achievements. Acknowledge and celebrate the closure of each loop. This recognition reinforces the positive feelings associated with completion and motivates you to continue.

The benefit of closing loops extends beyond mere task management; it affects your overall quality of life.

Consider the open loops in your personal life: the door that doesn't close properly, the leaky faucet, the cluttered garage. Left unresolved, these minor issues contribute to a pervasive sense of disorder and frustration. Addressing them creates a harmonious and functional living environment, fostering a sense of peace and well-being.

In life, closing loops significantly enhance productivity and career satisfaction. Unfinished projects and unmet goals are a source of constant stress, undermining your confidence and performance.

By systematically addressing these open loops, you streamline your workflow, improve efficiency, and create a clear path for advancement.

> Closing loops requires a psychological shift, moving from a mindset of procrastination and avoidance to one of proactive engagement and resolution.
>
> This shift is challenging but is ultimately transformative. It requires discipline, focus, and a commitment to personal growth.

Adopting this mindset means recognizing the value of completion and understanding that progress, in its fullest sense, is about finishing what you start. It's about bringing projects to fruition, achieving goals, and fully resolving tasks. This approach cultivates a sense of integrity and reliability—both in yourself and how others perceive you.

Life is full of open loops, both large and small. The key to harnessing momentum lies in your willingness to close these loops, complete what you start, and recognize the immense power of finished tasks. Doing so transforms your life from a state of fragmentation and disorder to one of coherence and fulfillment.

This is the essence of momentum: the relentless drive to move forward, grow, and achieve your fullest potential.

SECTION 2 ARTIFICIALLY CREATING MOMENTUM

It becomes a powerful motivator when you start to feel the momentum building and see yourself progressing in the right direction. Each achievement, no matter how small, reinforces your sense of purpose, inspiring you to show up each day with renewed enthusiasm and determination. You begin to recognize the value in every step you take, understanding that each brings you closer to your goals.

But when momentum slips, motivation can quickly drain away, replaced by doubt and hesitation. This is when we're most at risk of falling into patterns of inaction or even giving up entirely. In these moments, pushing back against stagnation is essential to shift your perception by consciously reigniting your drive.

> If momentum seems absent, this is precisely when you need to take bold action, even if it feels forced. By artificially creating momentum, you convince your mind you're back on track and progressing, even before the results are clear.

With this intentional push, you gradually spark real momentum. Over time, this builds a cycle of achievement that fuels itself, keeping you steadily moving toward your goals.

MOMENTUM PERCEPTION

*****

> Momentum plays a pivotal role in driving your actions. Yet, perhaps equally significant is the perception of momentum. How you interpret and internalize your progress, or lack thereof, significantly influences your willingness to continue striving for success.

The perception of momentum often sustains your drive and keeps you moving forward. When you genuinely believe you're making headway, even the most minor steps feel meaningful and contribute to your overall progress.

This belief boosts motivation and reinforces commitment to goals. You become more willing to tackle challenges and push through obstacles because you can see how far you've come.

On the flip side, experiencing a sense of stagnation creates a significant mental barrier that is difficult to overcome. You start to doubt your abilities and question whether your efforts are worthwhile. This feeling of being stuck is paralyzing, leading to a lack of action and further entrenching you in a cycle of inaction. By addressing these feelings and finding ways to create small wins, you shift your perception and reignite the momentum you need to move forward.

> Momentum perception refers to how you perceive the momentum you've built in your endeavors. It's not merely about your tangible progress but how you subjectively interpret it.
>
> When you feel momentum, you're more inclined to show up with enthusiasm and determination every day and view your efforts as purposeful.
>
> Conversely, when you perceive your momentum as stagnant or waning, you become hesitant to act, questioning the value of your endeavors and succumbing to doubt and inertia.

The danger of momentum perception lies in its potential to become a self-fulfilling prophecy. If you perceive your momentum as alive and thriving, you're more likely to continue taking consistent action, further fueling your progress.

However, the moment you perceive your momentum as dead, whether due to fatigue, disappointment, or uncertainty, you risk falling into a cycle of inaction and stagnation. In these moments of perceived stagnation, you must recognize the importance of challenging your perceptions and actively seeking to reignite your momentum.

One key factor influencing your perception of momentum is your daily experiences and outcomes. For instance, if you wake up feeling tired and unmotivated one day, it's easy to perceive your momentum as depleted, leading you to question whether your efforts are worth it. Similarly, if you fail to achieve the desired results or face setbacks, it's natural to doubt the efficacy of your actions and lose sight of the momentum you've worked so hard to build.

> However, it's crucial to understand that perceived momentum is not solely determined by external factors or outcomes. Instead, your mindsets and attitudes largely shape it. Even when you feel tired or uninspired, you choose how you perceive your momentum and whether you allow temporary setbacks to derail your progress.

By cultivating a growth mindset and reframing challenges as opportunities for growth, you maintain a positive perception of your momentum and continue moving forward with resilience and determination.

Moreover, perceived momentum underscores the importance of seeking momentum daily – actively creating and sustaining momentum in areas that matter to you. This means taking intentional actions daily to move closer to your goals, even if it's just one small step forward. By consistently making progress, however incremental, you reinforce your perception of momentum and build momentum over time, creating a virtuous cycle of success and achievement.

> Using the perception of momentum to your advantage involves recognizing the power of feeling progress, even when it's manufactured.
>
> When you cultivate an impression of forward motion, you reinforce a belief in your advancement, creating a mental framework where success feels imminent. By engaging in actions that foster this perception, you trigger a feedback loop in which your mind aligns with the idea of progress, fueling motivation and reducing the hesitancy to act.

This belief, even if initially artificial, instills a sense of purpose and commitment, as if you're already on a winning path, making it easier to stay engaged and pursue your goals. Ultimately, it's not about whether your momentum is real or perceived but rather about your willingness to show up each day and take meaningful steps toward your goals, one day at a time.

REHEARSING MOMENTUM

*****

Visualization can be a game-changer when it comes to creating momentum. But instead of picturing the result in broad strokes, try to get specific.

Imagine particular moments along your journey, milestones you'll hit, actions you'll take, and even small celebrations you'll have along the way. This detailed approach keeps you motivated and helps your brain feel closer to the finish line, giving you the boost you need to keep going.

Start by visualizing your progress in scenes. Imagine the steps that will take you from where you are now to where you want to be.

Let's say you're working toward launching a project: picture yourself sitting down to complete a significant part of it, like finishing the first draft or setting up your workspace for a productive day. Imagine sitting down, feeling focused, and the satisfaction of checking off each small step along the way. By picturing these detailed steps, the journey becomes more familiar and achievable. Instead of a distant, hazy goal, you're building a mental roadmap that feels like a path you've already traveled.

Next, envision those decisive moments when you hit key milestones. Picture yourself finally solving a tricky problem holding you back, hearing that first big "yes" from a client, or sending off a completed project.

Imagine the sounds and sights of these moments: the notification ding of that email sent, the deep breath of satisfaction, or even the proud smile on your face. Adding sensory details makes success feel immediate and real, fueling your confidence and motivation.

Affirmations strengthen this practice by connecting you emotionally to your goals. Imagine repeating affirmations like, "I am steadily moving forward," "I am capable of overcoming any obstacle," or "Every step brings me closer to my goal." Let the emotions sink in as you imagine the pride and satisfaction of achieving these small wins. You're teaching your mind to crave the experience of moving forward, even on tough days.

> Your brain loves familiarity, so by vividly rehearsing what success feels like, you're giving yourself a preview of it. The more real it becomes in your mind, the more naturally you start moving toward those scenes.

Finally, make this a daily habit. Spend a few minutes each morning or evening to picture your day's steps toward your goal. Visualize the small wins, the feelings of progress, and the pride in following your plan. Pair this with affirmations like, "I am on track to reach my goal," or "I am committed to taking action every day." With each visualization and affirmation, you create a feedback loop of motivation, reinforcing your momentum and grounding you in believing what you're working toward isn't just possible. It's happening, one step at a time.

CRAFTING EXCITEMENT

*****

When you find yourself trapped in a cycle of stagnation, it often feels like you have little to talk about with friends and family. The silence can be deafening, filled with the weight of unspoken disappointments and a sense of emptiness. You might feel ashamed, believing your life has become dull and unremarkable. This self-perception makes sharing your experiences daunting. Feeling stuck creates a vicious cycle: the less you have to share, the more isolated you become, reinforcing the belief that your life lacks excitement.

You must actively project yourself into a more dynamic narrative to break free from this stagnation. Start by acknowledging your life is exciting, even in the smallest ways. Shift your mindset from viewing life as mundane to seeing it as a canvas for exploration and discovery.

> This transformation begins with the commitment to find at least one thing each day that excites you, something worthy of sharing.

Begin this process by reverse engineering what you want to share. Consider the stories or experiences inspiring you. What makes you feel alive or curious? Perhaps it's trying a new hobby, exploring a local café, or diving into a book that sparks your imagination. By identifying these elements, you create a plan to incorporate them into your daily life. When you have something exciting to share, it doesn't just give you conversation starters; it fosters a sense of agency and purpose.

Instead of indulging in complaints about your stagnation, actively seek experiences that enrich your life. Challenge yourself to step outside your comfort zone, even if it's just a tiny step. Attend an event, join a class, or converse with someone new. The goal isn't necessarily to have grand experiences but to infuse your daily routine with little moments that ignite joy and curiosity.

As you gather these small experiences, you create a repertoire of stories and insights to share with others. This practice not only lifts the burden of feeling uninteresting but also opens the door to deeper connections. People are drawn to excitement and passion, and when you share your newfound experiences, it can inspire them to seek their own adventures.

Moreover, having something to share creates momentum in your life. Each exciting moment feeds into the next, generating a cycle of curiosity and engagement. As you express enthusiasm about your experiences, you cultivate a positive feedback loop. Your energy inspires others, and their responses encourage you to seek even more fulfilling experiences.

Life is not about waiting for extraordinary moments to happen; it's finding the extraordinary within the ordinary.

By consciously crafting exciting narratives in your life, you combat feelings of shame and stagnation and embrace the idea that every day holds the potential for something remarkable.

In this way, you create momentum for yourself and invite others to join you on a journey filled with excitement, exploration, and growth.

FEEDBACK LOOP DESIGN

*****

Designing a personal feedback loop is a game-changer when creating momentum artificially. Think of it as a system where you give yourself regular checkpoints and reflections so you can see your progress in real time. It's like building your own "proof of progress" that boosts confidence and reinforces your work, even when it's hard to see the significant results immediately.

Start with small, regular progress markers. This might mean setting daily or weekly reminders to jot down your accomplishments. You don't need to write essays; just a quick list of completed tasks or milestones. Did you write a few pages, make an important call, or organize a key part of your workspace? Capture it.

> These small acts might seem insignificant, but when they are stacked up, they create a sense of movement.
>
> Each small accomplishment contributes to the bigger picture, and writing it down allows you to pause, recognize, and appreciate the work you're putting in.

Visual trackers can also make your feedback loop more tangible. Some people like using a physical chart, a wall calendar where you mark each day you've made progress on your goal, or a simple checklist in a notebook. Apps can also work well for this, primarily if you're motivated by digital reminders and want to track patterns over time. Either way, each mark or check-off becomes a mini-celebration, a nod to yourself that you're moving forward, even when progress feels slow.

The real power of a feedback loop is that it builds momentum through accountability and reward. To amplify this, consider adding a small reward system. After completing a series of tasks or meeting a weekly milestone, give yourself a small treat, a coffee from your favorite spot, an episode of a show, or a relaxing break.

This doesn't just add a moment of enjoyment but connects your hard work to tangible rewards, making it more satisfying to stick with your plan.

Another aspect to consider is a "review and refine" routine. Every week or so, set aside a few minutes to monitor your progress and reflect on your feelings about it.

Notice where you're gaining momentum or you feel stuck and adjust accordingly. Maybe you'll realize that you're spending too much time on low-priority tasks or that a particular approach is working well and deserves more attention.

This self-check creates a loop where you notice your progress and stay flexible and responsive to what you need to keep moving forward.

When built intentionally, feedback loops transform how you work toward your goals. They make invisible progress visible, keeping you aware of every little movement you're making.

Over time, this accumulated awareness adds up, creating a growing sense of purpose, progress, and, most importantly, the motivation to keep going.

GET TO WORK

*****

You may think a lack of belief in yourself is holding you back, but what if that's not? What if it's not a mindset problem but simply the behaviors you keep repeating? You get trapped in your head, convinced that a lack of self-confidence is the main obstacle. You believe that if you could think your way out of it, find the proper perspective, or somehow shift your mindset, you could break through and reach success.

> But what if you didn't need to work so hard on your mindset to move forward? What if the key to progress lies in action, not intention?
>
> Momentum doesn't happen in your head. It occurs in the small, concrete things you do every day. Think of any moment when you felt genuinely accomplished or truly energized. It wasn't because you spent hours analyzing your goals or psyching yourself in the mirror. It was because you did something that shifted your day forward. You took an action that built the foundation for momentum.

It's easy to get stuck thinking, "I need more motivation" or "I have to believe in myself more."

But motivation isn't the driver—it's the passenger that comes along for the ride once you get moving. You get so wrapped up in waiting for the right feeling, the perfect mindset, or some bolt of confidence that'll suddenly change everything. But you're not wired to think yourselves into action; you're wired to act your way into a mindset shift.

So, get busy with your hands instead of spending time in your head. Want to write a book? Write a paragraph, even if it's not perfect. Want to get fit? Start with ten minutes of exercise today, not with researching the best routine. Small actions add up, and they're much more powerful than the finest-tuned self-belief could ever be. This isn't to say that confidence or belief in yourself isn't necessary. It is, but it's a natural byproduct of what you do, not something you think into existence.

Imagine standing at the edge of a pool, telling yourself you'll jump in as soon as you feel ready. But here's the catch: readiness is a myth. You're never going to feel entirely prepared. Confidence doesn't come from waiting; it's earned in the doing. Every time you take action, even imperfect, you prove to yourself that you're capable. And each small action builds on the last, creating a ripple effect that pulls you out of stagnation and into momentum.

So, take one step forward today, whatever that looks like for you—no need to wait for the perfect mindset or conditions. Just get moving. When you shift your focus from what you feel to what you do, you'll start to see things happening. You'll build the momentum that no amount of inner pep talk can give you. With each small action, you might build the self-belief you thought you lacked.

> So, take the plunge. Let your actions define you, not your thoughts. Let your hands get busy, and watch as your life transforms. The journey out of stagnation doesn't start in your head; it starts with your next move.

YOUR NEXT STRATEGIC MOVE

*****

One of the most powerful ways to initiate and sustain momentum in your life is by identifying and pursuing your next strategic move. This concept revolves around recognizing your open loops and selecting the one that will lead to the most progress and is realistically achievable within a few months, an objective that excites you.

The strategic move is not necessarily your ultimate dream but a significant, attainable goal that sets the stage for further success.

Defining the Strategic Move

A strategic move is a goal you feel confident you can achieve but still find somewhat challenging and exciting. It should be ambitious enough to stretch your abilities but not so lofty that it becomes overwhelming or unattainable.

The key is balancing ambition with practicality, ensuring the goal is within reach, given your current resources and circumstances.

> Often, the next strategic move is not your grand vision for your life but a stepping stone to it.
>
> Focusing on a definitively possible goal builds confidence and momentum, which you can leverage to tackle more substantial challenges in the future.

Steps to Identify Your Next Strategic Move

Assess your current open loops, unfinished tasks, goals, and projects.

Identify which ones seem to be progressing the most substantially.

Understanding where you are and what you have already achieved helps you see where to go next.

- **Balance ambition with practicality.** Choose a goal that excites you and is also within your current capabilities. It should be something you can realistically achieve within a few months. Avoid setting goals that are too lofty or out of reach, leading to frustration and demotivation.
- **Consider your long-term vision.** While your strategic move should be attainable, it should align with your broader aspirations. It should be a stepping stone to your ultimate goals, contributing meaningfully to your long-term vision.
- **Evaluate the impact.** Consider the potential impact of achieving your strategic move. Will it significantly improve your life, health, career, or relationships? The more substantial the effect, the more motivated you will pursue it.
- **Seek excitement and challenge.** Your strategic move should be exciting and challenging. It should push you out of your comfort zone, but not so much that it becomes overwhelming. The right level of challenge will keep you engaged and motivated.

Implementing Your Strategic Move

Once you have identified your next strategic move, commit to it fully. Here are some steps to help you achieve your goal:

- **Set clear, specific goals.** Define your goal in clear, specific terms. For example, instead of saying, "I want to get fit," specify, "I want to reduce my body fat to 15% by September."
- **Create a plan.** Develop a detailed plan to achieve your goal. It should include actionable steps, timelines, and milestones. This might involve a workout schedule, a nutrition plan, and regular progress tracking for a fitness goal.
- **Stay consistent.** Consistency is crucial. Stick to your plan, even when your motivation wanes. Remember, progress is often gradual and requires sustained effort.
- **Monitor progress.** Track your progress and adjust your plan as needed. Regularly reviewing your progress helps maintain motivation and ensures you stay on track.
- **Seek support.** Surround yourself with supportive people who encourage and motivate you. This could be friends, family, a coach, or an online community.
- **Celebrate achievements.** Celebrate your milestones and achievements to reinforce the positive behavior and motivate you.

The Benefits of the Strategic Move

Pursuing a strategic move offers many benefits. It provides a sense of direction and purpose, helping you avoid the paralysis of having too many open loops. It builds confidence and self-efficacy, creating a positive feedback loop that fuels further progress. Additionally, it leads to unexpected opportunities and growth, as each achievement opens new doors and possibilities.

While fitness goals are an excellent starting point, the strategic move concept can be applied to any area of life. The principles remain the same whether you're advancing in your career, building stronger relationships, or achieving personal development goals.

For instance, if your goal is to advance in your career, identify a skill or certification that will significantly impact your performance and make it your strategic move. Focus on this goal for the next few months, investing time and effort into achieving it. This focused effort leads to a promotion, a new job opportunity, or enhanced job satisfaction.

In relationships, a strategic move might involve improving communication skills or spending more quality time with loved ones. Set specific, achievable goals, such as having a meaningful conversation with your partner every day or planning a weekly date night.

THE POWER OF BASICS

*****

Creating momentum might seem impossible when you're at rock bottom and desperate, stuck in a place where you're unsure how to take even the smallest step forward. You may feel lost, exhausted from trying to find solutions, and questioning what your next move should be. In times like this, the answer isn't to overthink or try to map out a grand strategy. The answer is to pull back and focus on the basics. Forget the complex solutions and the need to figure everything out right now. Instead, take a deep breath and embrace the simplest tasks in front of you. Start building, brick by brick, from the ground up.

When life feels overwhelming, and you can't see a clear path, the basics can serve as your compass. These fundamental small habits, routines, and incremental tasks may feel insignificant, but they provide the stability you need to regain your footing. They're your foundation, and they're where actual growth begins.

This isn't about avoiding the problem. It's about realizing that sometimes the fastest way forward isn't by trying to solve everything at once but by grounding yourself in manageable actions. These basics, even if they seem mundane or unremarkable, are the building blocks of resilience. By focusing on them, you build momentum and nurture the strength and consistency you'll need to tackle bigger challenges later. In this approach, there's no pressure to make monumental changes or grand leaps. Instead, there's a calm, deliberate focus on simple, doable actions.

Show Up Daily, Even When It's Hard

Momentum isn't found in the occasional brilliance or the big, life-changing moments. It's built into the everyday routines and choices that might feel repetitive or boring. When you're desperate, the last thing you might feel like doing is something ordinary. But these ordinary, everyday actions are where you'll find the momentum to start moving again.

This means showing up daily, regardless of how motivated or uninspired you feel. On the days when everything feels overwhelming, you might not want to push forward. That's normal. But instead of thinking about the entire journey, narrow your focus to just today. Maybe all you can manage today is a small task like organizing your workspace, drinking a glass of water, or writing down one goal for tomorrow. No action is too small to be the start of something greater.

> Momentum is born out of consistency, not extraordinary bursts of effort. Don't fall into the trap of waiting until you feel inspired to act. Instead, act first and let momentum grow naturally from there. Often, you'll find that the more you show up, the easier it becomes to keep showing up.

The Value of Routine

It's tempting to think that the answers to your challenges lie in radical solutions or groundbreaking ideas. You can find most of what you need by committing to a steady, simple routine. A consistent routine may feel limiting, especially if you're struggling, but it's a way to regain control over your life.

When you're lost, routines bring structure. They remove the need to constantly make decisions, freeing up mental energy for things that matter. Even as simple as making your bed, drinking water, or spending a few quiet minutes gathering your thoughts, a morning routine can ground you in the present moment. These small, almost unremarkable actions might not solve your biggest problems immediately, but they build a foundation of calm and stability that allows you to think more clearly.

Routines might sound boring, but that's also their strength. In the repetition, you'll find comfort and confidence. And you're creating a small victory every day you stick to your routine. These victories compound over time, turning your routine into a source of strength.

Growth Happens Slowly, Not Overnight

It's natural to crave a quick fix or immediate relief when desperate. But here's the truth: growth and change don't happen overnight. They result from continuous, small efforts made over an extended period. The basics teach you patience and resilience because they require you to keep going, even when you don't see immediate results.

Sometimes, focusing on the basics feels frustrating because the rewards aren't instant. You might find yourself wondering if these small actions are making any difference. But remember, growth is often invisible until one day, suddenly, you notice the results. Like a plant that grows slowly beneath the soil before sprouting, your efforts are taking root even if you can't see them yet.

SECTION 2 ARTIFICIAL MOMENTUM

> So, as you embrace the basics, allow yourself to trust the process. Avoid the temptation to check your progress or constantly search for shortcuts. Success, especially in challenging times, is rarely linear. Trust that you create a stable path that will eventually lead to lasting change by focusing on foundational actions.

When you're feeling lost, it's tempting to try everything at once, hoping that something will work. However, this scattered approach often creates more confusion and frustration. Instead, simplify. Strip away anything unnecessary and focus only on the essentials. Ask yourself: What basic actions will move me forward, even if only slightly? These actions don't need to be groundbreaking or complex. Sometimes, the most straightforward choices have the most profound impact.

Keeping it simple isn't about avoiding the hard work; it's about removing distractions. You don't need to have all the answers to start making progress. All you need is to commit to small, manageable steps that feel attainable.

Focusing on a few simple actions gives you the mental space to see things more clearly. Over time, these simple actions create momentum, making it easier to take on more complex challenges when the time comes.

In the Mundane, You Find Your Power

> If there's one thing to remember when building momentum from a place of desperation, it's this: you don't find momentum in the extraordinary; you see it in the mundane. It's in the daily grind, the monotonous repetition of basic tasks, and the unwavering commitment to doing what needs to be done, regardless of how unglamorous it may seem.

When you embrace the basics, you're laying a solid foundation for the future. These simple actions might not solve all your problems instantly, but they create stability, focus, and direction. In the process, you're building the resilience to keep going, no matter what comes your way. So, when you're feeling lost, you don't need a grand plan or perfect motivation to start. All you need is a commitment to the basics. The momentum will follow.

SECTION 3 PRIMING MOMENTUM

When you prime your momentum, you transform how you approach your goals and daily activities. Priming momentum involves creating conditions that foster a continuous and positive flow of energy and progress. Just as an engine needs a spark, your actions and mindset need specific triggers to activate and sustain forward movement. By intentionally setting up these triggers, you overcome inertia and ensure that you consistently direct your efforts at achieving your aspirations. This approach is about working harder and more intelligently, harnessing the power of small, deliberate actions to generate and maintain momentum.

> Imagine waking up daily with purpose and direction, knowing that each step you take propels you closer to your goals. Priming momentum is about cultivating that feeling and making it a daily reality.

It starts with recognizing the activities, habits, and environments that energize and motivate you. Integrating these elements into your routine creates a supportive framework that naturally encourages progress. Whether it's a morning ritual that sets a positive tone for the day, achieving small wins that build confidence, or surrounding yourself with a motivating community, priming momentum ensures you always move forward. This strategic approach to momentum significantly enhances productivity, resilience, and overall satisfaction in both personal and professional realms.

MORNING MOMENTUM

*****

When we talk about momentum, we're referring to the drive, energy, and productivity that propels us forward. It's that feeling of being in the zone where tasks flow effortlessly and progress comes naturally.

> However, the challenge arises when you realize your momentum doesn't simply carry over from one day to the next. The natural slowdown during sleep disrupts the flow, requiring us to start fresh each morning. This disruption can be frustrating, as it often feels like you're perpetually rebuilding your momentum from the beginning.

Imagine runners in a relay race. Each time they pass the baton to the next runner, there's a slight pause before the next sprint begins. Similarly, when you go to sleep, you pass the momentum baton to your rested selves, but there's a gap between the end of one day and the start of the next, and that's where momentum wanes.

This phenomenon raises a question: How can we bridge this gap and maintain momentum for continuous progress? Momentum isn't solely dependent on external factors like workload or deadlines. Internal factors such as mindset, motivation, and energy levels influence it.

> One effective strategy is pre-sleep preparation. By taking time at the end of each day to reflect on your accomplishments and set intentions for the next day, you mentally prepare yourself to hit the ground running when you wake up. This might involve jotting down a to-do list for the following day or visualizing your goals and priorities.

Establishing a bedtime routine promotes relaxation and mental clarity and eases the transition from wakefulness to sleep. Activities such as reading, journaling, or practicing mindfulness signal to your brain that it's time to wind down, making it easier to drift into restful slumber.

Once you wake up, morning rituals help kick-start your momentum for the day. Engaging in physical activity, such as a morning jog or yoga session, boost your energy levels and sharpen your focus. Similarly, setting clear goals and priorities for the day provides a sense of direction and purpose, guiding your actions and decisions.

Imagine starting your day with a series of affirmations to fuel your success. These affirmations are not just words; they are your guiding light, your roadmap to greatness, infusing your morning with energy, positivity, and purpose.

Picture yourself waking up, ready to conquer the world, and instead of reaching for your phone, you take a few deep breaths and focus on your intentions for the day. You might also start with mindfulness practice, centering yourself and creating a calm, focused mindset. Both options set the tone for everything that follows, allowing you to approach the day with clarity and determination. As you move into physical activity, whether it's a brisk morning jog, an energizing yoga session, or a quick workout, pair these movements with your affirmations.

Reciting statements like "I am strong and full of energy" or "I embrace challenges with enthusiasm" while exercising boosts your physical energy and primes your mind for a successful day.

Hydration is key. Drinking a glass of water rehydrates your body and kick-starts your metabolism. Following this with a nutritious breakfast fuels your body and mind, providing sustained energy for the day ahead. Opt for foods rich in nutrients, such as oatmeal, fruits, eggs, or nuts, avoiding sugary options that lead to energy crashes. As you nourish your body, continue with affirmations like "I fuel my body with healthy choices" to reinforce positive habits.

> Creating a morning to-do list further solidifies your momentum. Spend a few minutes jotting down the top three priorities for the day. This helps organize your thoughts and provides a clear roadmap for your actions.

Knowing your most essential tasks gives you a sense of direction and purpose, enabling you to approach your day with intention and focus. Integrate affirmations such as "I am focused and productive" or "I achieve my goals with ease" to bolster your determination and drive.

Reflecting on your long-term objectives is incredibly motivating. Think about your bigger goals and how your daily actions contribute to achieving them. This reflection keeps you connected to your overarching purpose, maintaining your motivation even during routine or mundane tasks. Affirmations like

"Every step I take brings me closer to my dreams" reinforce this connection and sustain your daily momentum.

Personal development is another essential aspect of a powerful morning routine. Engage in activities that stimulate your mind and encourage growth, such as reading a motivational book, listening to an inspiring podcast, or journaling your thoughts and ideas.

These practices enrich your mind and set a positive, proactive tone for the day. Pairing these activities with affirmations like "I am constantly growing and evolving" or "I embrace new knowledge and experiences" enhances their impact and sets you up for success.

Finally, practicing gratitude transforms your mindset. Spend a few moments each morning reflecting on what you are grateful for. This simple practice shifts your focus from what you lack to what you have, fostering a positive and appreciative mindset.

Studies have shown gratitude improves mental well-being, enhances mood, and increases overall life satisfaction. Affirmations such as "I am grateful for the abundance in my life" or "I appreciate the small moments of joy" amplify this practice, creating a firm foundation for your day.

> To sum up, establishing a morning routine that includes physical activity, hydration, nutritious eating, affirmations, goal-setting, personal development, and gratitude creates a powerful start to your day. By incorporating these elements into your morning routine, you build immediate momentum to carry you through the day with confidence and enthusiasm.

While the natural slowdown during sleep may disrupt your momentum, it's not an insurmountable obstacle. By understanding how momentum works and implementing effective strategies to sustain it, you can bridge the gap between days and maintain consistent productivity and progress. With dedication and mindfulness, you can keep the momentum going and continue moving closer to your goals.

HISTORY REPEATS ITSELF

*****

The saying "history repeats itself" captures the idea that our actions and choices today often shape our actions and choices tomorrow.

> Patterns formed over time create pathways in our behavior, leading us to repeat familiar actions in similar situations.
>
> This concept illustrates a fundamental truth: we tend to keep doing what we've just done. Our recent actions become not only reflections of our habits but also strong indicators of our future decisions.

This idea of repetition and pattern recognition is crucial for building momentum. Consistency becomes the engine that drives forward movement, transforming isolated bursts of energy into lasting progress and meaningful growth.

Feeling motivated for a day or two is easy, but consistency turns this short-lived enthusiasm into something sustainable. By dedicating time each day, whether it's an hour to work on a personal project, a few minutes to practice a new skill or a half-hour for a workout, you're completing individual tasks and weaving habits into the fabric of your life. Over time, these habits develop into momentum, propelling you forward without needing constant motivation.

Consider a simple example: getting up early each morning, lacing up your running shoes, and hitting the pavement for a jog. At first, it may feel like a forced effort, something you push yourself to do. But as the days pass, the action becomes a natural part of your routine. You're not just running but building momentum, one jog at a time. What was once a struggle becomes a habit, fueling a steady rhythm of progress.

Momentum, at its core, is powered by repeated action. Each consistent step you take reinforces your commitment to your goals, making it easier to stay on track. By incorporating these actions into your daily routines, you're establishing habits that reduce resistance and make it easier to keep moving forward. In doing so, you create a cycle: the more you practice consistency, the easier it becomes to maintain momentum and reach your objectives.

Ultimately, when you focus on repeating positive actions, you create a self-sustaining growth cycle. Consistency in one area can inspire growth in others as the habits you build spill over into new aspects of your life. Momentum is about reaching a goal and creating a lifestyle of continuous progress. Through daily actions, even small ones, you can leverage the power of repetition to break down big goals into achievable steps, bringing you closer to your vision one day at a time.

CREATE HABIT LOOPS

*****

Habits are like invisible threads woven into the fabric of your daily lives, guiding your actions and shaping your behaviors in subtle and profound ways. At the heart of every habit lies what psychologists call the habit loop—a simple yet powerful framework that explains how habits form and how you maintain them.

At its core, the habit loop comprises three key components: cue, routine, and reward. Each element plays a crucial role in shaping your habits and ultimately determining the direction of your momentum journey.

Cue. The cue serves as the trigger that activates the habit loop. It can be anything from a specific time of day to a particular location to an emotional state to even other people. Cues prompt you to engage in particular behaviors and become the starting point for your habitual routines.

Routine. The routine is the behavior—the action or series of actions you perform in response to the cue. This is the part of the habit loop you're most familiar with, as it's what you actively engage in daily. Whether hitting the snooze button when the alarm goes off or reaching for a snack when stressed, your routines are the tangible manifestations of your habits.

Finally, you reach the reward—the positive reinforcement you receive from completing the routine. Rewards take many forms, from physical sensations like pleasure or relief to emotional states like satisfaction or fulfillment.

Whatever the reward, it reinforces the habit loop and increases the likelihood that you'll engage in the same behavior again.

As you repeat the habit loop, the neural pathways in your brain strengthen, making it easier and more automatic for you to engage in the behavior.

This process, known as neuroplasticity, allows habits to become deeply ingrained in daily routines and influence behavior over time.

But here's where it gets interesting: by recognizing the role of habits in your momentum journey, you strategically design your routines to propel you forward with greater ease and efficiency.

Instead of being at the mercy of your habits, you control them and use them to your advantage.

Designing Routines

So, how do you design routines that support your momentum journey? It starts with understanding the cues that trigger your habits and the rewards that reinforce them.

First, identify the cues prompting you to engage in specific behaviors. Is it a certain time of day? A particular location? An emotional state? A specific event? By pinpointing the cues triggering your habits, you become more aware of when and why you engage in certain behaviors.

Next, examine the routines following these cues. Do they help or hinder your progress? If they lead you away from your goals, it may be time to consider replacing them with more positive alternatives.

Finally, consider the rewards you receive from completing these routines. Do they truly fulfill your needs and desires, or do they provide temporary satisfaction? By identifying the true rewards driving your habits, you focus on behaviors that align with your long-term goals and aspirations.

MOTION CREATES MOMENTUM

*****

> Motion creates momentum. But there's no momentum without motion. It's a concept deeply rooted in the laws of physics—the idea that an object in motion stays in motion while an object at rest remains stagnant.

Beyond its scientific implications, this principle holds profound significance in our lives. It speaks to the transformative power of action. By taking consistent, purposeful steps toward your goals, you start a chain reaction of progress and growth that propels you to success.

> Momentum is being in the flow, where everything falls effortlessly into place. But what many fail to realize is that momentum doesn't just materialize out of thin air. You create it through deliberate and sustained motion.

Think of it like pushing a boulder up a hill. At first, it takes tremendous effort to get the boulder moving. But as you continue trying, building momentum with each step, the task becomes more manageable, and the boulder gains speed. Before you know it, you're riding the wave of momentum propelled by the force of your actions.

But motion isn't just about taking a big leap—it's about taking consistent, purposeful action every day. It's about establishing habits and routines that keep us moving, even when going is tough.

A breakthrough is the catalyst that initiates the momentum.

Alex, a beginner swimmer, has practiced tirelessly for months. Yet his technique feels clunky, and his progress is slow. He feels like he's hitting an invisible wall, unable to break through to the next level. Each stroke is a struggle, each lap a reminder of his stagnation.

One day, during a particularly intense training session, something shifted for Alex. He had worked with his coach on refining his stroke, focusing on reducing resistance and maximizing efficiency. Then, it happened in the middle of a lap—an effortless glide through the water. For the first time, he experienced slicing through the pool with minimal effort, the water parting smoothly around him. This was his breakthrough moment.

This breakthrough is not merely a minor improvement; it's a profound shift in his technique and mindset. The gears of progress turn within Alex. The glide is not just a physical experience but a mental revelation. He has tapped into a new level of efficiency and speed, realizing that what once seemed impossible is within his grasp.

Fueled by this breakthrough, Alex begins a new phase of momentum in his training. He becomes more motivated, his confidence soars and his progress accelerates. From this point forward, every training session builds on the techniques he has learned. The initial breakthrough ignites a chain reaction of continuous improvement. Alex's time drops and his stamina improves. The glide he once experienced occasionally becomes a consistent feature of his strokes. The initial effort to reach the breakthrough was monumental, but the subsequent momentum carried him to new heights he had not imagined possible.

> This story illustrates the profound impact a breakthrough has on your life. It highlights how an initial perspective, technique, or understanding shift sets the stage for significant, sustained progress. It underscores the importance of persistence and the willingness to push through periods of stagnation, trusting that the effort will eventually lead to that pivotal moment of breakthrough.

In your life, you often face periods where progress seems elusive, and your efforts feel futile. It is during these times that you must remember the power of breakthroughs. The moment everything clicks can transform your trajectory, initiating a powerful momentum that propels you forward. By embracing the challenges and persisting through difficulties, you position yourself to experience these transformative moments, ensuring that you continually progress in your journey of growth and achievement.

QUANTUM LEAP DAYS

*****

> Sometimes, the ordinary effort isn't enough. Enter quantum leap days—specific days where you push yourself to achieve extraordinary work or training far beyond your usual output. These days are intense bursts of productivity, akin to making a "quantum leap" in your progress.

These days have a transformative impact. They significantly advance your goals and create a powerful sense of accomplishment that fuels further momentum.

SECTION 3 PRIMING MOMENTUM

In martial arts, intense, all-encompassing training sessions are often called gasshuku in Japanese. Gasshuku, "training camp" or "intensive training," is where practitioners gather to undergo rigorous, concentrated training over a short period. Gasshuku encapsulates the essence of quantum leap days, where athletes focus on pushing limits, building skills, and fostering a deep sense of accomplishment and growth.

Imagine waking up with a clear, unwavering intention to make today different. This isn't just another day on the calendar; it's a quantum leap day, where you push your boundaries and redefine what you believe is possible. For an athlete, this could mean an intense marathon training session or participating in back-to-back competitions. The idea is to test and expand your limits to see how far you go when you give it your absolute all.

On a quantum leap day, you start early, perhaps with a grueling workout that sets the tone for the day. The adrenaline pumps through your veins as you push your body harder than before. Every muscle tenses, each breath is controlled, and your mind is fully locked in on the task. The physical challenge is immense, but the sense of progress, of pushing past your usual limits, is exhilarating. Each rep, each lap, and each mile becomes a testament to your commitment and drive.

But quantum leap days aren't just about physical exertion. They also demand a high level of mental discipline and focus. You might dedicate a day to tackling the most challenging aspects of your work, the tasks requiring deep concentration and sustained effort. It's a time to push through mental barriers, solve lingering problems, and make significant strides in your projects.

> The intensity of these days leads to breakthroughs that would otherwise take weeks or months to achieve.

The appeal of quantum leap days is their ability to break the monotony and create a sense of urgency and purpose. When you dedicate a day to achieving extraordinary results, you disrupt your routine and force yourself to operate at peak efficiency. The sheer intensity of these days leads to a profound sense of accomplishment. You end the day exhausted but with deep satisfaction that you pushed yourself to the edge and achieved something remarkable.

For athletes, the benefits of quantum leap days are particularly potent. Engaging in marathon training sessions or back-to-back competitions builds physical endurance, strength, and mental toughness. It teaches you how to manage fatigue, stay focused under pressure, and find that extra gear when you think you've got nothing left. These days simulate the demands of competition, preparing you both physically and mentally for the challenges ahead.

Moreover, the momentum gained from such intense efforts is incredible. After a quantum leap day, you might find subsequent training sessions or workdays easier by comparison. The progress made during these fierce periods creates a ripple effect, boosting your confidence and motivation in the following days and weeks. Each quantum leap day builds on the last, creating a cycle of continuous improvement and momentum.

> Quantum leap days should not be every day; they are unique, infrequent events that demand high preparation and commitment. They require you to clear your schedule, minimize distractions, and approach the day with a laser-focused mindset. The rewards, however, are youll worth the effort. By dedicating specific days to push yourself beyond your usual limits, you can make significant leaps in your progress and achieve a sense of accomplishment that fuels further momentum.

Embrace the challenge. Push yourself harder, achieve more, and see how these bursts of effort can transform your journey to success.

THE BUGENHAGEN METHOD

*****

The Bugenhagen method is one of the most effective ways to harness and sustain momentum. Named after Eric Bugenhagen, a powerlifter and wrestler whose unconventional approach to fitness applies to virtually any area of life, this method involves focusing intensely on a single task until you reach a plateau and then switching to a new focus.

Eric Bugenhagen's philosophy is straightforward yet profoundly effective. Unlike traditional training programs that cycle through various exercises and rep schemes, Bugenhagen picks one exercise and performs it relentlessly until he no longer sees progress. This approach eliminates the distraction of too many goals and homes on one objective with a laser-like focus.

The Bugenhagen method does not only apply to fitness. It's a universal strategy for driving momentum in any area of life. Whether mastering a skill, advancing in your career, or achieving personal goals, the key is to identify one significant task or an open loop to focus on exclusively until you reach a plateau.

Here are the steps:

Identifying Your Focus

The first step is pinpointing where concentrated effort will yield the most meaningful progress. This goal should genuinely matter to you and make a substantial difference in your life. It might be a skill, a habit, or even a creative project. The goal should be clear and achievable within a few months of intense effort.

Blasting It into the Ground

Once you've identified your focus, commit to it with everything you've got. You'll need to work on your task daily, pushing yourself to make incremental improvements. This isn't about gradual, comfortable progress but a relentless pursuit and sustained effort.

For instance, if you aim to become proficient in a programming language, immerse yourself in it. Allocate daily hours to coding, completing projects, and solving problems. To improve public speaking, join a club like Toastmasters, practice speeches daily, solicit feedback, and refine your techniques. This method also permits you to temporarily neglect less critical areas of your life.

> By channeling most of your energy into one task, you'll achieve breakthroughs much faster than if your efforts were scattered.

Embracing the Plateau

Inevitably, you'll hit a plateau. In fitness, this might mean no longer increasing weight or reps. In other pursuits, it could mean reaching a skill level where progress slows down noticeably. This is not a sign of failure but a natural part of the process. It signifies that you've squeezed out most of the easy gains and reached a new proficiency baseline.

When you hit this point, it's time to switch focus. Choose a new goal or task that builds on your created momentum. This could mean moving from learning one programming language to another or from public speaking to advanced negotiation skills. The skills and confidence gained from your first focused effort will make tackling the next goal more effective.

One of the most significant advantages of the Bugenhagen method is the psychological boost it provides. Focusing on one task eliminates the overwhelming challenge of juggling multiple goals. The satisfaction of daily progress and the clear markers of achievement keep you motivated and engaged.

This method leverages the power of habit and consistency. Working on the same task daily builds a routine ingrained in your lifestyle. This habitual effort leads to compounded gains and sustained momentum.

The Bugenhagen method is a powerful strategy for initiating and sustaining momentum in any area of life. By choosing one meaningful goal, focusing intensely on it, and pushing through until you plateau, you can achieve remarkable progress quickly.

This method encourages deep commitment to your goals, providing a clear path to mastery and significant achievement. Whether you're lifting weights, advancing your career, or pursuing personal growth, the principles of the Bugenhagen method transform your approach and propel you to success.

SECTION 4 STEERING MOMENTUM

Experiencing momentum is one of the most exhilarating sensations in life—those moments when everything clicks and the gears of progress turn.

Imagine effortlessly gliding in a swimming pool's calm, cool waters. Each stroke feels stronger than the last, your body cutting through the water with power and grace. You're fully in sync with the water, which seems to carry you as you push harder, driven by focus and determination. Your breathing and movements fall into a natural rhythm, creating a smooth, fluid motion as you swim. With every pull, you edge closer to your goal, and the excitement of the chase fuels your energy, urging you to keep going. Victory is within reach, and nothing can stop you now.

In the pool, as in life, momentum is a powerful force that propels you toward your goals with unwavering determination. With each stroke, you build upon your successes and push past your limitations, driven by the relentless pursuit of excellence. And as you glide through the water, the exhilarating rush of momentum builds, bringing you closer to your dreams.

This forward motion isn't just a fleeting thrill for athletes—it's a visceral confirmation that you're on the right path and that your hard work and dedication are paying off in tangible progress.

Momentum isn't just reserved for the elite athletes competing on the world stage. It's a fundamental aspect of human nature, deeply ingrained in your psyche, essential for your overall well-being.

Just as a runner gains momentum with each stride, so do you experience momentum in your daily life, whether making progress on your fitness goals, advancing in your career, or cultivating fulfilling relationships.

THE FIRST LAW OF PHYSICS

*****

The concept of momentum, often discussed by physicists, applies just as powerfully to your life.

Momentum is the force that propels you forward once you initiate movement. It keeps you pushing through challenges and helps you achieve continuous improvement.

> But what if you find yourself stuck in a rut, lacking the momentum others seem to harness effortlessly?
>
> If you lack positive momentum, it's probably because you've never tried cultivating it.

Momentum isn't a mere concept.

The first law of physics, also known as Newton's first law of motion or the law of inertia, states an object will remain at rest or in uniform motion in a straight line unless acted upon by an external force. In simpler terms, objects maintain their current state of motion, staying still or moving at a constant velocity unless an applied force changes that motion.

This law forms the foundation of classical mechanics and is essential for understanding the behavior of objects in the physical world. Momentum is the product of two key factors: mass and velocity.

> Momentum = Mass × Velocity
>
> Mass refers to the amount of matter within an object, while velocity is the speed and direction of its motion. Together, these components determine the object's overall momentum.

A simple analogy illustrates the concept of momentum: imagine a freight train barreling down the tracks at high speed. The train's massive size and high speed give it significant momentum, enabling it to move through obstacles effortlessly.

Momentum is a force of nature, like a river coursing through rugged terrain. Its potential is immense—it carves majestic canyons or wreaks havoc when untamed. Just as a river needs banks to channel it, momentum requires direction to unleash its power for good.

Without purpose, momentum is like a boulder careening down a mountainside, bouncing off obstacles, and causing chaos.

Imagine a sprinter racing down the track, every step fueled by raw energy. Without a clear finish line in sight, that energy is wasted and dissipates into thin air. It's the same with momentum in your life. Without purposeful direction, it's just scattered bursts of power leading nowhere.

Yet, within this chaos lies an opportunity to harness momentum's raw force and steer it to your goals.

It's a delicate balance, like navigating a ship through stormy seas. You must chart a clear course, knowing where you want to go and how to get there. Only then can momentum work in your favor, bringing you closer to your dreams with each step forward. You must lead your momentum with determination and focus like a coach guiding their team to victory.

Steering momentum is a skill—a rhythm between power and purpose. It requires clarity of vision, commitment to action, and the courage to navigate the twists and turns of life's journey.

> So, how do you use momentum?
>
> Start by identifying your goals and aspirations, the destinations where you can direct your momentum.
>
> Your goals will most likely appear in your open loops, those unresolved tasks and ambitions lingering in your mind.

Whether you're launching a new business, pursuing a passion project, making positive changes in your life, or participating in athletic endeavors like improving your time in a race, having a clear sense of direction is essential for harnessing momentum.

PURPOSE-DRIVEN

*****

Being purpose-driven is about aligning your choices and actions with your core values. It requires you to dig deep and understand what truly matters to you, guiding you to make decisions that resonate with your deepest aspirations and beliefs. Instead of external influences or passing whims swaying you, being purpose-driven means you tap into an inner compass that leads to decisions in harmony with your authentic self.

> This approach is instrumental in building momentum and providing a clear sense of direction. When you ground yourself in your values and purpose, you have a roadmap for where you want to go and how to get there.

This clarity is a guiding light, helping you navigate through life's twists and turns with confidence and conviction. Whether navigating career choices, relationship decisions, or personal pursuits, having a clear purpose empowers you to make choices that align with your long-term vision and aspirations.

Being purpose-driven infuses your actions with meaning and significance. When your choices align with your values and purpose, you experience a profound sense of fulfillment and satisfaction. Each decision becomes an opportunity to live out your values and contribute to something larger than yourself. Whether it's making a positive impact in the lives of others, pursuing a passion project that lights you up, or striving for a better world, aligning with your purpose fuels your commitment and dedication to your goals.

When grounded in your purpose, setbacks become temporary detours rather than insurmountable obstacles. Your sense of purpose provides the resilience and determination to overcome adversity, learn from your experiences, and keep pressing forward. During moments of uncertainty, your purpose is a source of strength and inspiration, reigniting your passion and refocusing your efforts on your goals.

Being purpose-driven becomes a catalyst for progress and growth. When you align your actions with your values and purpose, you create a powerful synergy that enhances your efforts.

Each decision becomes a building block, contributing to the momentum generated by previous choices and laying the groundwork for future achievements. Whether you're pursuing a new career opportunity, launching a business venture, or embarking on a journey of personal growth, being purpose-driven accelerates your progress and enables us to unleash your full potential.

Acting with integrity means embodying your true self in every decision. This authenticity boosts your credibility and trustworthiness, strengthens your connections with others, and fosters meaningful relationships and collaborations that support your journey to success.

When purpose guides your actions, you get a sense of inner alignment and harmony, which translates into increased confidence, resilience, and overall well-being.

SCENARIO ANALYSIS

*****

Scenario analysis is like having a crystal ball that glimpses into the future, helping you anticipate challenges, capitalize on opportunities, and navigate uncertainty with precision. This strategic mindset is crucial for directing momentum effectively. It acts as a roadmap to success, providing a structured approach to navigating the uncertainties and challenges within a competitive environment. The proactive nature of scenario analysis empowers one to anticipate obstacles and capitalize on opportunities before they arise.

> Rather than reacting to unforeseen circumstances, you can take a proactive approach to strategize your next move. This enables you to stay one step ahead of the competition and maintain momentum in your pursuit of success.

One key benefit of scenario analysis is its ability to identify the most promising paths forward. Examining various scenarios, you assess the potential risks and rewards associated with each course of action. This allows you to make informed decisions aligned with your goals and objectives. Whether it involves adjusting your approach, refining your techniques, or seeking strategic partnerships, you leverage scenario analysis to identify the most effective strategies for success.

By gaining a deeper understanding of the potential outcomes of your decisions, you ensure that you are moving in the right direction. This clarity enables you to maintain focus and momentum as you work to achieve your goals.

At its core, scenario analysis is about envisioning possibilities and preparing for what lies ahead. This means exploring a spectrum of potential outcomes, from triumphant successes to unforeseen setbacks and everything in between. It's about understanding the landscape of your field, recognizing the ebbs and flows of competition, and charting a course that maximizes your chances of success. With each scenario you examine, you gain clarity and insight, empowering you to make informed decisions and stay focused on your aspirations.

But scenario analysis offers more than just foresight—it's a catalyst for strategic innovation and growth. Imagine honing your skills, your mind alive with creative possibilities. Through scenario analysis, you uncover hidden opportunities, identify emerging trends, and devise innovative strategies that give you a competitive edge.

Scenario analysis fosters a culture of continuous improvement and learning. Whether faced with challenges or unexpected obstacles, you draw upon your scenario analysis toolkit to pivot, adapt, and move toward your goals. By regularly evaluating different scenarios and their outcomes, you identify areas for improvement and refine your strategies accordingly.

Scenario analysis is a masterclass in strategic thinking and decision-making. It's like a mental gymnasium where you exercise your cognitive muscles, honing your ability to think critically, plan strategically, and execute with precision. By examining different scenarios and considering their potential implications, you develop a strategic mindset that serves you both on and off the field. Whether it's weighing the risks of a bold strategy or seizing an unexpected opportunity, you approach every decision with confidence and conviction, knowing that you have the foresight and preparation to succeed.

Scenario analysis is more than just a tool—it's a mindset, a way of approaching the world with curiosity, foresight, and resilience.

BACKWARD MOMENTUM

*****

Backward momentum and inertia are forces affecting your progress, but they operate in distinct ways.

Understanding the difference is crucial for navigating life's challenges and steering yourself to success.

Inertia is a state of inactivity or resistance to change. It's when you find yourself stuck, unable to initiate movement in any direction.

This lack of motion is due to various factors, such as fear of failure, lack of motivation, or not knowing where to start.

Inertia is like a heavy anchor that keeps you stationary, preventing you from progressing.

> Backward momentum, on the other hand, actively pulls you away from your goals. Unlike inertia, characterized by a lack of movement, backward momentum involves movement in the wrong direction.
>
> It's a negative cycle in which efforts seem to backfire, and every step taken feels like a step further from your objectives.

Backward momentum results from repeated failures, poor decision-making, or external setbacks. It stalls progress and undoes it, creating a compounding effect that is demoralizing and difficult to reverse.

The impact of backward momentum is profound.

Consider a scenario where you have trained rigorously for a competition but then experience a series of injuries. Each injury hampers your performance and erodes your confidence and motivation. You might fear pushing yourself, leading to hesitant and ineffective training sessions.

This negative spiral results in deteriorating performance, where one fails to improve and sees a decline in one's abilities.

> The mental toll of backward momentum is just as debilitating as the physical, causing doubt and anxiety to overshadow your original drive and passion.

Recognizing negative momentum is the first step in reversing it. Recognizing the signs of negative momentum and taking deliberate actions to halt its progress reset the stage to a neutral state of inertia. Signs include consistent setbacks, declining performance, loss of motivation, and feelings of frustration or defeat. For an athlete, this might manifest as slower race times, increased frequency of mistakes, or a noticeable drop in enthusiasm for training sessions.

> It's essential to take a step back and reassess the situation to shift from inertia to forward momentum. This involves acknowledging the negative trends and understanding their root causes.

Shifting from backward momentum to inertia means halting the negative cycle. For an athlete, this could involve taking a break to recover from injuries fully, seeking professional guidance to correct training techniques, or addressing mental health issues affecting performance.

Once you've stopped the negative movement, the next goal is building positive momentum.

This starts with setting small, achievable goals that create a sense of accomplishment and rebuild confidence. Gradually increasing the intensity and frequency of training, celebrating small wins, and maintaining a positive outlook are crucial.

Engaging with a supportive community, such as coaches, teammates, or mentors, provides the encouragement and accountability needed to maintain momentum.

COURSE CORRECTION

*****

When we think of momentum, we often imagine moving forward at full speed, fueled by determination, vision, and energy. We picture unstoppable force—a train barreling down the tracks, a wave crashing toward the shore, or a sprinter breaking through the finish line. While this imagery is powerful, it can also mislead us into thinking that success requires constant, unrelenting acceleration.

> Momentum isn't about always moving full power in the direction you first envisioned; it's about having the wisdom and flexibility to make small course corrections along the way. These minor adjustments ensure you stay on track, maintain your progress, and adapt to changing circumstances without stalling or veering entirely off course.

Things rarely go exactly as planned in life, business, or personal development. Circumstances shift, unexpected obstacles arise, and sometimes, our initial vision no longer aligns with reality. Yet momentum doesn't have to come to a screeching halt when these changes occur.

By embracing the art of recalibration—small, intentional shifts—you can steer your momentum and keep progressing toward your goals. The beauty of course corrections is that they don't require you to start over or abandon your journey; they involve making minor changes to ensure you're still heading in the right direction.

Imagine you're piloting a ship. Your destination lies far beyond the horizon, and you're moving steadily across the open sea. However, the ocean is not a static environment. Waves, winds, and currents constantly push and pull your ship off course. If you ignore these forces, even the slightest deviation could lead you miles off target. A successful navigator doesn't panic or radically change direction at every small shift. Instead, they make minor, consistent adjustments to steer the ship back toward its intended path.

This same principle applies to steering momentum in your life or work. When people encounter challenges or distractions, they often feel the need to overcorrect—to make sweeping, dramatic changes. However, massive changes can disrupt your momentum entirely, causing confusion, wasted energy, and unnecessary stress. Instead, focusing on minor course corrections keeps you moving forward while staying aligned with your ultimate vision.

For example, if you're working toward a business goal and realize that a particular strategy isn't yielding results, the solution isn't always to scrap everything and start over. Instead, you might tweak one element: adjust the messaging, explore a slightly different target audience, or refine your timeline. These small, deliberate changes allow you to adapt while maintaining the momentum you've already built.

Adaptability is the secret weapon of those who maintain momentum over the long haul. The world constantly changes—markets shift, technology evolves, people grow, and unexpected challenges arise. If you remain fixed on a single path or refuse to adjust, you risk falling stuck or behind.

> Being adaptable doesn't mean abandoning your vision. It means being open to finding new, creative ways to achieve it. Think of it as driving on a winding road: you may need to turn the steering wheel left or right to navigate curves, but you're still moving toward your destination. Minor course corrections allow you to flow with changes rather than resist them.

This flexibility also helps you stay resilient. When setbacks occur, adaptable people don't see them as failures; they see them as opportunities to adjust and improve. They understand that maintaining momentum is less about perfection and more about perseverance—about finding ways to keep moving, even if the path looks different than initially imagined.

Momentum doesn't require perfection nor demand an unyielding commitment to a single plan. It thrives on flexibility, self-awareness, and the ability to make small, intentional course corrections. By pausing to assess, implementing incremental changes, and staying adaptable, you can steer your momentum in the right direction—even when the journey takes unexpected turns.

> Remember, the path to any worthwhile goal is rarely linear. What matters most is not how straight the path looks but how steadily you move forward.
>
> Small shifts, recalibrations, and adjustments are not signs of weakness; they are marks of wisdom and resilience. Embrace them, and you'll discover that maintaining momentum is not about powering through at all costs but about steering yourself skillfully toward success.

MOMENTUM MAPPING

*****

Momentum mapping is a game-changer, harnessing the dynamic power of technology to propel you to your aspirations.

> At its core, momentum mapping involves using digital tools or apps to input goals and desired outcomes. It generates a visual roadmap that illuminates various scenarios and strategies, effectively steering momentum in the right direction.

The true strength of momentum mapping is its ability to provide real-time feedback and invaluable suggestions for course corrections.

This tool continuously updates the roadmap, seamlessly adapting to any obstacles or shifts in circumstances. This adaptive feature empowers athletes to remain laser-focused and agile, ensuring they remain steadfast on their path to success.

Consider a young swimmer eager to elevate their performance. Armed with a momentum mapping app, they set their sights on ambitious goals: slashing their lap times and enhancing their endurance.

With a few taps on their device, a comprehensive roadmap unfolds, brimming with tailored training strategies and key milestones.

As they dive into their training regimen, the app becomes their ever-vigilant coach, delivering real-time feedback and insightful suggestions for refining their approach.

Should they encounter hurdles—a stubborn plateau or an unexpected injury—the app swiftly offers strategic course corrections, enabling them to adapt and conquer challenges head-on while maintaining their momentum to excellence.

In the absence of digital tools, there are myriad alternative methods for visualizing goals and tracking progress.

From the simplicity of pen and paper to the sophistication of spreadsheets, you can craft customized tracking systems tailored to your unique needs and preferences.

Whether scribbling aspirations in a journal or creating a vibrant vision board adorned with motivational images, the key lies in embracing a tangible representation of your goals, anchoring your vision firmly in reality.

> While momentum mapping provides a valuable framework for goal setting and progress tracking, it's essential to complement this approach with mentoring to gain perspective and ensure the momentum is heading in the right direction.

Mentoring involves partnering with a seasoned athlete or coach who provides guidance, support, and accountability.

Mentoring offers several benefits in conjunction with momentum mapping.

First, mentors provide valuable insights and advice based on their experiences and expertise to avoid common pitfalls and mistakes and navigate challenges more effectively. Additionally, mentors provide encouragement and motivation to stay focused and resilient in the face of setbacks.

> Furthermore, mentors offer a fresh perspective on goals and strategies, helping you ensure your momentum is heading in the right direction. By discussing your goals and progress with a mentor, you gain valuable feedback and insights and identify areas where your training regimen may need adjustment.

For example, returning to the young swimmer, imagine they have an experienced coach. They meet regularly to discuss progress, analyze training routines, and brainstorm solutions. The mentor offers guidance on technique improvement, helps the athlete stay focused on long-term goals, and provides encouragement and support.

Combining momentum mapping with mentoring creates a powerful synergy that maximizes your chances of success.

SECTION 5 SEIZING OPPORTUNITIES

Opportunities are all around us, waiting to be discovered and leveraged. But it's not enough to stumble upon them by chance. To spark momentum, you must actively seek opportunities and be prepared to seize them when they present themselves. Recognizing the right moment and seizing those opportunities as they arise is the spark that ignites momentum.

Think of opportunities as kindling for the fire of momentum. Each one has the potential to fuel your progress and propel you closer to your goals, but it's up to you to recognize them, see the potential they hold, and take decisive action to capitalize on them.

EMBRACE THE SIDE QUEST.

*****

Life often resembles a high-octane race, much like the adrenaline-fueled world of the *Ultimate Racer* video game. Like in the game, where players chase victory in exhilarating races, your real-life goals feel like the ultimate race for success. But like in *Ultimate Racer*, there are side quests—smaller, less daunting challenges that provide unexpected benefits and propel you to your primary objectives.

The primary goal in *Ultimate Racer* is to dominate the streets, win races, and build a reputation as the top racer. However, the game has side quests—tuning cars, completing challenges, and taking on rival crews. These tasks may not be as flashy as winning races, but they offer valuable rewards, such as better performance, new customization options, and increased respect from fellow racers.

In the same way, you have your main goals: landing a dream job, starting a successful business, or achieving financial independence. These goals feel overwhelming, like trying to win the most challenging race in *Ultimate Racer*.

> But just as in the game, side quests provide a way to build momentum and make progress, even when the primary goal seems out of reach.

Similarly, pursuing your primary goals in Ultimate Racer is a thrilling but challenging journey. It requires skill, strategy, and persistence. But sometimes, the main quest feels like an uphill battle, with obstacles and setbacks slowing your progress. In those moments, turning to side quests provides a much-needed boost. For example, if your main goal is starting a successful business but struggling to get it off the ground, you might focus on side quests like networking, honing your skills, or gaining industry experience. These tasks may not directly lead to success in the main quest, but they provide valuable insights, connections, and resources to help you achieve your goals.

> Side quests are not distractions—they are opportunities for growth and learning.

In *Ultimate Racer*, tuning your car or completing challenges may not be as exciting as winning races, but they significantly impact your performance on the track. Similarly, side quests like learning skills, building relationships, or taking on new challenges may not seem directly related to your primary goals. They provide valuable experiences, insights, and connections.

One of the most powerful aspects of side quests is their ability to provide micro wins—small, achievable goals that boost confidence and momentum. In *Ultimate Racer*, winning races may be the goal, but completing challenges, earning respect from rival crews, or unlocking customization options provide a sense of progress and satisfaction to keep you motivated to continue racing.

Similarly, achieving small victories like mastering a skill, overcoming a challenge, or progressing on a side project provides the momentum and confidence you need to keep pushing toward your goals.

Just as in *Ultimate Racer*, the journey to success in life is as important as the destination. Side quests add depth and excitement to the journey, making it more enjoyable and fulfilling. In the game, tuning your car, exploring new routes, and taking on challenges may not directly contribute to winning races, but they add variety and excitement to the experience. Similarly, pursuing side quests like learning skills, building relationships, or exploring opportunities makes the journey to your goals more enjoyable and fulfilling.

Strategic Use of Side Quests

While side quests are valuable, it's essential to use them strategically. They should support your goals rather than distract from them. Here are some strategies for making the most of side quests:

1. Identify relevant side quests. Choose side quests that align with your main goals and provide valuable benefits. For example, if your goal is to start a business, side quests like networking, honing your skills, or gaining industry experience provide useful insights and connections.

2. Set clear objectives. Define what you want to achieve with each side quest and how it contributes to your primary goals. For example, if your main goal is to start a business, a side quest like networking might involve attending industry events, connecting with potential mentors, or joining professional groups.

3. Balance and timing. Use side quests strategically to complement your main goals and keep momentum. For example, if facing challenges or setbacks in your main quest, focusing on side quests provides a much-needed boost and helps you stay motivated. However, it's essential to strike a balance and not let side quests distract you from your primary goals.

4. Reflect and adjust. Regularly assess your progress and adjust your side quests as needed. If a side quest doesn't contribute to your main goals or provide the benefits you expected, it may be time to reevaluate and focus on other tasks that will move you closer to success.

In life, as in *Ultimate Racer*, side quests offer valuable opportunities for growth, learning, and progress. While the main quest may be the ultimate goal, side quests provide valuable experiences, insights, and connections that ultimately help you succeed. By embracing side quests, setting clear objectives, and using them strategically, you can build momentum, overcome challenges, and ultimately achieve your goals.

READY FOR THE UNEXPECTED

*****

While pursuing momentum, one principle stands out: meticulous preparation. This isn't just a matter of working hard but also of working smart and staying vigilant for the right opportunities. The concept of preparation transcends the mere honing of skills and knowledge; it encompasses a mindset of continuous improvement and an unwavering readiness to seize the moment when it presents itself.

Imagine an athlete tirelessly training day after day. Every early morning run, every grueling practice, and every minute spent refining technique is an investment in future success. This dedication ensures when an unexpected opportunity arises—a last-minute spot in a major competition, for example—the athlete isn't just ready but poised to excel. The athlete's peak physical condition and sharpened skills allow them to step in confidently, perform spectacularly, and gain recognition that might have otherwise been out of reach.

> This readiness is not born out of luck but a deep commitment to preparation.

The same principle applies across all fields and professions. Consider a musician practicing their instrument for hours daily, learning new pieces, and staying updated on industry trends. When a sudden opportunity to audition for a prestigious orchestra or band arises, they don't catch them off guard. Instead, they step up to the plate, confidently perform, and potentially secure a life-changing position. Their preparation transforms what could have been a daunting challenge into a well-deserved victory.

> Preparation is not merely about skill acquisition but about staying informed and adaptable. Awareness of potential opportunities and threats is crucial in a constantly changing world.

For instance, a business professional who continuously updates their industry knowledge, attends relevant conferences, and engages in networking is more likely to recognize and act on emerging trends. When a new market opportunity or groundbreaking technology appears, they pivot their strategy and leverage their preparation to gain a competitive edge.

You can see this readiness mindset in how tech entrepreneurs operate. They are always looking for the next big thing, constantly learning about advancements in their field, and anticipating market shifts. When disruptive technology emerges, they don't start from scratch. Instead, they have the foundation of knowledge and skills to innovate and adapt quickly. This ability to harness preparation allows them to turn potential disruptions into opportunities for growth and success.

Meticulous preparation helps build resilience and adaptability. Life is unpredictable, with inevitable setbacks. However, those who are well-prepared navigate these challenges more effectively. An athlete who trains rigorously recover from an injury faster because they have a strong physical and mental foundation. Similarly, a professional with a diverse skill set and knowledge base pivots more easily when faced with career challenges or industry changes.

Preparation also involves strategic foresight. It's about envisioning various scenarios and being ready for them. A chess player who anticipates their opponent's moves and prepares counter-strategies stays several steps ahead, ready to capitalize on any mistakes and adapt to changing circumstances. In the business world, this translates to having contingency plans and being prepared to seize opportunities that align with your goals.

Preparation means setting clear goals and breaking them into actionable steps. It involves regular self-assessment and course correction. For instance, someone aiming to become a published author might start by setting a daily writing routine, attending workshops, and seeking peer feedback. Over time, these small, consistent efforts build, and when the opportunity to publish arises, they are ready to take it confidently.

The power of preparation extends to mental readiness as well. Visualization and mental rehearsal are techniques top performers across various fields use. Athletes often visualize their performance before a competition, mentally performing each move and anticipating possible scenarios. This mental preparation builds confidence and reduces anxiety, allowing them to perform best when it matters most.

Similarly, mentally preparing for important meetings, presentations, or negotiations can make a significant difference in professional settings.

Visualizing success, anticipating questions or objections, and rehearsing responses enhance performance and outcomes. This mental preparedness ensures that you deliver with poise and precision when the spotlight is on.

Another critical aspect of preparation is developing a strong support network. Surrounding yourself with mentors, coaches, and peers who provide guidance, feedback, and encouragement is invaluable. For an athlete, this might mean having a coach who pushes you to your limits and helps you refine your technique. In a professional setting, it could be a mentor who shares their wisdom and experience, helping you navigate your career path more effectively.

In essence, preparation is the bedrock of momentum. It empowers you to recognize and seize opportunities, navigate challenges with resilience, and maintain a trajectory of continuous improvement. It transforms life's unpredictable nature into manageable, actionable steps.

An athlete who trains tirelessly, a musician who practices relentlessly, and an entrepreneur who stays ahead of trends embody the principle that success is not a matter of chance but a result of unwavering preparation.

As you embark on your journey to momentum, remember that every moment spent preparing is an investment in your future. The foundation allows you to capitalize on opportunities, adapt to changes, and overcome obstacles. Embrace the power of preparation, and you'll be ready to seize the moment and achieve your aspirations with confidence and determination.

MAKING TIMELY DECISIONS

*****

Recognizing opportune moments isn't just about being in the right place at the right time—it's also about making timely decisions.

> Hesitation is costly. The longer you wait to act, the greater the risk of missing out on valuable opportunities.

Decisiveness is the fuel that powers momentum. It's about trusting your instincts, weighing the risks and rewards, and making bold decisions in uncertainty. When you act decisively, you set the momentum wheels in motion, propelling yourself forward with confidence and purpose.

Capitalizing on the Right Moment to Act

Seizing opportunities and making timely decisions are only part of the equation. To spark momentum, it would be best to capitalize on the right moment to act. This means recognizing when an opportunity is ripe for the taking and having the courage to seize it with conviction.

Capitalizing on the right moment to act requires a combination of foresight, intuition, and calculated risk-taking. It's about seeing a potential for success where others see only obstacles and having the courage to pursue it relentlessly.

So, how does recognizing opportune moments link with sparking momentum? It's simple: each opportune moment you seize and each timely decision you make catalyzes momentum. Like sparks igniting a fire, these moments of action and decisiveness set off a chain reaction of progress and growth.

> When you seize an opportunity, you create momentum. When you make a timely decision, you fuel momentum. When you capitalize on the right moment to act, you propel momentum forward with unstoppable force.

By seizing opportunities as they arise, making timely decisions, and capitalizing on the right moment to act, you set yourself up for success and ensure momentum is always on your side. So, don't wait for opportunities to come—create them yourself.

THE RHYTHM OF SUCCESS

*****

Timing is the heartbeat of momentum. Just as a martial artist is in tune with the rhythm of the match, you must align your actions with the ebb and flow of your goals.

There's a saying in martial arts: "Timing overcomes strength." It means even a smaller opponent can overcome a larger one by striking at the perfect moment. In your momentum journey, recognizing the opportune moment is equally transformative. It involves seizing opportunities as they arise, making timely decisions, and capitalizing on the moment to act.

> The rhythm of success is not a monotonous beat but a dynamic interplay of pulsing and pacing.

In this complex process, timing and execution drive progress and achievement. With its intense effort and energy bursts, pulsing propels you with short, powerful strides. It's the adrenaline-fueled sprint that breaks barriers and sets new benchmarks. On the other hand, pacing provides the steady, enduring cadence that sustains your journey over the long haul. The measured, deliberate march ensures you maintain your stamina and focus.

> Together, pulsing and pacing form the heartbeat of success, each rhythmically contributing to the momentum that transforms goals into reality.

Pulsing

Pulsing is a powerful and dynamic concept that revolutionizes how you approach your goals and maintain momentum. By alternating between periods of high-intensity effort and intervals of rest or low-intensity activity, pulsing leverages your body's natural energy systems to maximize performance and sustain forward motion. Understanding how pulsing relates to momentum provides valuable insights into optimizing performance in fitness and daily life.

The physiological foundation of pulsing lies in the body's energy systems, which supply energy differently depending on the duration and intensity of physical activity.

For example, the phosphagen system provides immediate energy for short, high-intensity efforts but depletes quickly.

The glycolytic system, however, kicks in during moderate to high-intensity activities, breaking down carbohydrates to produce adenosine triphosphate (ATP).

Meanwhile, The oxidative system is the primary energy source for prolonged, low-intensity activities, converting carbohydrates, fats, and proteins into ATP.

Pulsing uses these systems by alternating high-intensity bursts with recovery periods, enhancing anaerobic and aerobic capacities.

Momentum in athletics is more than just physical progress; it combines physical, psychological, and emotional factors that create an unstoppable forward motion. Pulsing plays a crucial role in building and maintaining this momentum through several mechanisms. By engaging in high-intensity intervals, athletes push their physical limits, increasing their overall performance. These bursts of effort stimulate muscle growth, cardiovascular efficiency, and metabolic rate, contributing to greater athletic prowess. The rest intervals allow the body to recover partially before the next high-intensity effort, reducing overall fatigue and enhancing the ability to sustain momentum over extended periods.

Pulsing also repeatedly challenges athletes to push through discomfort and fatigue, helping to build their mental toughness and resilience. This mental fortitude is essential for maintaining momentum as athletes learn to cope with intense efforts and recover quickly, fostering a mindset of continuous improvement. The varied nature of pulsing workouts prevents monotony, keeping athletes engaged and motivated. This variety stimulates physical and mental adaptation, reducing the risk of burnout and maintaining their drive to persist.

Athletes achieve short-term goals more frequently by breaking down training into manageable, high-intensity segments. These minor victories contribute to a sense of progress and accomplishment, fueling long-term momentum toward larger goals.

Beyond athletic training, you can use the principles of pulsing to see benefits in various aspects of your lives. In professional settings, you can apply pulsing to work routines to enhance productivity and prevent burnout. You maintain high concentration levels and efficiency throughout the day by alternating between focused work periods and short breaks.

SECTION 5 SEIZING OPPORTUNITIES 121

> The Pomodoro Technique is a popular pulsing method where you work intensely for 25 minutes, then take a 5-minute break, repeating this cycle. This technique helps you manage time effectively, reduce mental fatigue, and sustain momentum in achieving work-related goals.

To implement pulsing effectively, follow these guidelines: define clear goals, plan intervals, monitor progress, prioritize recovery, and stay engaged. Establish specific, measurable, achievable, relevant, and time-bound (SMART) goals to provide direction and purpose. Design a pulsing routine that includes well-defined high-intensity efforts and recovery periods. Track your performance and progress regularly, using metrics such as time, distance, repetitions, or heart rate to assess improvement and make necessary adjustments to the pulsing routine.

Incorporate adequate recovery periods to prevent overtraining and reduce the risk of injury.

Incorporate different exercises, drills, or activities to keep the pulsing routine varied and enjoyable, maintaining motivation and avoiding boredom.

Pulsing is a powerful concept that leverages the body's natural energy systems to build and sustain momentum. By alternating between high-intensity efforts and recovery periods, you enhance performance, improve recovery, build mental resilience, and stay engaged.

Whether applied to athletic training, professional work routines, or daily life, pulsing provides a structured approach to achieving goals and maintaining momentum. Adopting the principles of pulsing leads to tremendous success, fulfillment, and overall well-being.

Pacing

The timing of each step while executing a plan profoundly affects overall momentum. This concept is especially pertinent to athletes. Much like in a product development cycle, where timely feedback loops and iterative testing phases sustain momentum through continuous improvement, athletes must meticulously manage the pacing and cadence of their training and competition schedules to maintain and build their performance momentum.

For athletes, maintaining the right pacing and cadence is akin to orchestrating a symphony where every note and rest contributes to the masterpiece. This begins with a structured training regimen that balances intensity, recovery, and progression. Athletes should time each training phase strategically to build upon the previous one, ensuring their performance peaks at the right moments.

Consider the training schedule of a marathon runner. The runner's training plan has distinct phases: base building, increasing mileage, speed work, tapering, and recovery. They must execute each phase with precise timing. During the base-building phase, the runner builds endurance through long, steady runs. The timing here is crucial, laying the foundation for more intense training sessions. Rushing through this phase or extending it too long leads to injury or a plateau in performance.

As the training progresses to increasing mileage and speed work, the timing of workouts and rest days becomes even more critical. The athlete can make necessary adjustments by incorporating timely feedback loops, such as regular performance assessments and physiological monitoring. If the athlete notices a decline in performance or an increase in fatigue, they adjust their training intensity or duration to prevent burnout and maintain forward momentum.

The tapering phase, where the athlete reduces training volume to allow their body to recover and reach peak performance, is another example of where timing is everything. A well-timed taper enhances performance by ensuring the athlete is well-rested and at their physical best on race day. Conversely, a poorly timed taper leaves the athlete feeling sluggish or not fully recovered, hindering performance.

Beyond training, pacing and cadence also apply to competition strategies. In sports like cycling or swimming, athletes must carefully time their efforts within a race. Going too hard too early leads to exhaustion, while a slow start may result in lost opportunities. Athletes must gauge their pacing, using feedback from their bodies and split times to adjust their efforts dynamically throughout the race.

A swimmer in a 1500-meter freestyle race must pace themselves to ensure they have enough energy to sprint in the final laps. They must execute the timing of their stroke rate, breathing, and turns flawlessly to maintain momentum and outpace competitors. This requires physical conditioning, strategic planning, and real-time adjustments based on how the race unfolds.

Moreover, athletes often undergo iterative testing and refinement of their techniques and strategies. Much like product development cycles, they use practice sessions, smaller competitions, and simulations to test new approaches and make adjustments. This iterative process helps fine-tune their performance, ensuring they optimize each step for the next.

> By avoiding long periods of inactivity between competitions or training phases, athletes keep their skills sharp and their competitive drive intact.

In team sports, the concept of pacing and cadence extends to the entire season. Coaches and players must plan the season's schedule, including games, practices, and rest periods, to ensure they peak at the right time—typically during playoffs or championships. This involves managing the intensity and volume of training, considering players' physical and mental fatigue.

Regular feedback from games and practices helps coaches make real-time adjustments to tactics and training loads, ensuring the team maintains its momentum throughout the season.

For individual athletes, maintaining engagement and drive also involves setting and achieving short-term goals that build long-term objectives. Each training session, competition, and recovery period is a step toward a larger goal, such as qualifying for the Olympics or setting a personal best.

> By maintaining a steady cadence and timely execution of their training plans, athletes keep their motivation and focus sharp.

Proper pacing and cadence are vital for athletes to build and sustain momentum. The timing of each step in training and competition plans affects their overall performance trajectory. Athletes maintain engagement, drive, and peak performance by incorporating timely feedback loops, making real-time adjustments, and avoiding prolonged inactivity.

Whether through structured training phases, strategic race pacing, or season-long planning, athletes who master the art of timing set themselves up for success, ensuring their momentum carries them to their ultimate goals.

Another critical aspect of pacing and recovery cycles is understanding your body's natural rhythms, often circadian rhythms. These physical, mental, and behavioral changes follow a twenty-four-hour cycle, responding primarily to light and darkness in your environment. Aligning work and rest periods with these natural rhythms enhances performance and well-being.

For example, many people experience peak cognitive function in the late morning, making this an ideal time for high-intensity tasks. Conversely, energy levels typically dip in the early afternoon, suggesting this is a good time for lighter tasks or a brief rest period.

Sleep, a fundamental recovery process, is crucial in maintaining overall health and productivity. While asleep, the body repairs tissues, consolidates memories, and restores energy levels. Therefore, prioritizing adequate and quality sleep is crucial to recovery cycles. Chronic sleep deprivation impairs cognitive function, reduces productivity, and increases the risk of various health issues. Establishing a consistent sleep schedule and creating a restful sleep environment significantly improve overall performance and well-being.

IMPULSIVE ACTION

*****

Mastering the balance of strategic patience and impulsive action is an art form. It requires an understanding of when to wait and when to leap. It's a tightrope walk, where the ability to discern the perfect moment to act transforms a mere opportunity into a defining triumph.

In a world that glorifies quick wins and immediate gratification, you often undervalue strategic patience. However, those who understand its power know that waiting is a form of preparation.

> Strategic patience is about recognizing that not every opportunity is right, and sometimes, the best action is inaction. This doesn't mean passivity or complacency but biding your time, gathering resources, and honing skills.

In contrast, there is a place for impulsive action; moments when hesitating can mean missed opportunities. The business world is filled with examples of entrepreneurs who seized a fleeting chance and reaped immense rewards.

> While patience is a virtue, seizing the moment with full commitment can be equally critical. It's about recognizing the signs, trusting your instincts, and taking bold steps when the time is right.

Balancing these two approaches requires deeply understanding your goals and the environment. It demands a keen sense of timing and the ability to read the landscape accurately. Strategic patience involves constant vigilance, always ready to pivot from waiting to action instantly.

It's a dynamic process in which you weigh each decision carefully against the broader context.

> The interplay between patience and impulsivity is evident, where predators like lions perfectly exhibit this balance. They spend hours, even days, stalking their prey, waiting for the perfect moment to strike. When that moment arrives, they act with explosive speed and precision. Their success hinges on their ability to wait for the right opportunity and act without hesitation.

You can cultivate this balance through mindfulness and self-awareness in your personal and professional lives. By understanding your tendencies and biases, you can better judge when to hold back and when to push forward. Strategic patience involves planning and forethought, while impulsive action demands confidence and decisiveness.

Consider a stock market investor. The patient investor studies market trends, understands the underlying value of companies, and waits for the perfect opportunity to buy low and sell high. But when the market shifts unexpectedly, presenting a rare chance to make a bold move, impulsive action, backed by strategic patience and deep knowledge, can lead to substantial gains.

This balance is also crucial in creative pursuits. A writer might spend years gathering experiences, researching, and honing their craft, waiting for the right story. They must act quickly when inspiration strikes, capturing the moment's energy and translating it into words. Their success lies in their ability to combine the patience of waiting for the right idea with the impulsiveness of diving headfirst into the writing process when it comes.

In relationships, too, balance is vital. Patience allows us to build deep, meaningful connections, taking the time to understand and appreciate the other person. Yet, there are moments when impulsive actions—grand gestures or spontaneous adventures—can strengthen the bond and create unforgettable memories.

The key to mastering this balance lies in listening to oneself and the environment. It requires tuning into the subtle cues, signaling when to wait and when to act. It's about cultivating a mindset that values patience and action, understanding they are not mutually exclusive but complementary.

This balance is particularly important for leaders. Effective leadership requires knowing when to give the team time to develop ideas and solutions and when to push for quick decisions and actions. Leaders who can navigate this balance create environments where innovation and efficiency thrive.

In sum, the balance between strategic patience and impulsive action is a powerful tool in pursuing success. It involves the wisdom to wait for the right opportunities and the courage to seize them when they arise. By mastering this balance, you position yourself to act with purpose and precision, transforming potential into reality. Whether in sports, business, personal growth, or relationships, this dynamic interplay guides you to achieve your highest aspirations.

> It is not a single act that sustains momentum but a series of actions and decisions that build on each other. This is where the interplay between patience and impulsivity becomes critical.

Strategic patience allows for the accumulation of energy and resources, while impulsive action ensures you use these resources effectively when the right opportunity arises. Together, they create a cycle of preparation and execution, where each phase feeds into the next, maintaining and accelerating momentum.

Building and maintaining momentum is about understanding the ebb and flow of action and preparation. It's about knowing when to harness a moment's energy and when to step back and prepare for the next surge. This balance creates a sustainable cycle of growth and achievement, where each phase supports and enhances the other.

Therefore, mastering the balance between strategic patience and impulsive action is key to building and sustaining momentum in every field, whether athletics, business, creative pursuits, or personal development.

This balance allows for the accumulation and effective use of resources, the ability to capitalize on opportunities, and the resilience to recover from setbacks. Understanding and applying this balance creates a powerful, sustainable momentum that drives continuous progress and success.

SECTION 6 SUSTAINING MOMENTUM

PLAN FOR PERIODIC RESETS

*****

You imagine momentum as a constant, upward trajectory, a steady push to your goals. Yet, the reality is momentum isn't always sustainable in a linear fashion. It ebbs and flows, much like the tides, and sometimes, it halts. This isn't a sign of failure; it's a natural part of any endeavor. Understanding and embracing this fact can transform how you perceive your progress and, ultimately, how you achieve your goals.

Imagine you're driving a car on a long, winding road. There are moments when you can speed ahead smoothly and others when you have to slow down for sharp turns or stop entirely at a red light. Life is much like this drive.

Momentum can be interrupted by various factors – burnout, unforeseen obstacles, changes in circumstances, or simply the need for rest.

Instead of seeing these interruptions as setbacks, what if you view them as necessary pauses that allow us to recalibrate, reflect, and rejuvenate?

> Acknowledging losing momentum is natural is the first step to a healthier, more sustainable approach to growth. This perspective shift is crucial. It alleviates the pressure to maintain a constant high and reduces the guilt of slowing down.

When you accept it's expected to pause, you permit yourself to step back without self-criticism. This pause can become a powerful tool for resetting. A reset period isn't about abandoning your goals or admitting defeat but strategic withdrawal to gain strength.

Think of it as when a runner stops to catch their breath, ensuring they can finish the race more decently and efficiently. During this time, you can evaluate what's working, what isn't, and why you lost momentum in the first place.

Are you overwhelmed? Have your goals shifted? Are external factors impacting your progress?

By addressing these questions, you can gain clarity and realign your strategies with your current reality.

> Moreover, resets provide space for creative thinking and problem-solving. When you're constantly moving, there's little room for reflection. Pausing allows your mind to wander to explore new ideas and perspectives, which is often when breakthroughs happen.

Many significant innovations and solutions have emerged not from a place of relentless pursuit but from quiet reflection and a change of pace. It's also essential to incorporate rest and recovery into your routine proactively. Just as athletes have off-seasons to recuperate, you, too, need periods of rest to avoid burnout.

These planned pauses can prevent forced halts caused by exhaustion or stress. Regular breaks, whether through vacations, hobbies, or simple downtime, ensure you consistently replenish your energy and enthusiasm.

When you view losing momentum as an opportunity for a reset, you transform the narrative from failure to strategic growth. It's a chance to step back, breathe, and return with renewed vigor. This cyclical movement pattern and rest creates a sustainable rhythm, allowing for continuous, long-term progress. Embracing this concept fosters resilience, adaptability, and a deeper understanding of oneself.

Ultimately, life is a marathon, not a sprint. Maintaining momentum doesn't mean slowing down; it means knowing when to pace yourself when to push forward, and when to rest. By accepting the natural ebb and flow of momentum, you can approach your goals with a balanced mindset, ensuring each step, whether fast or slow, brings you closer to your desired destination. This acceptance sustains your momentum and enriches the journey, making every pause as meaningful as every stride forward.

SEEKING ADVENTURE

*****

In the relentless pursuit of goals and the often monotonous grind of daily routines, it's easy to find yourself stuck in a rut. Your momentum wanes, enthusiasm dims, and the spark that once fueled your endeavors disappears. When this happens, the best action might not be to push harder or force yourself through the slump. Instead, stepping away and trying something completely different can be incredibly rejuvenating.

> Embracing new activities and experiences can reignite curiosity and enthusiasm, offering a fresh perspective and renewed energy for your original pursuits.

Imagine the mind as a garden. Tending to the same plants day in and day out can lead to neglect and lack of growth. However, introducing new seeds and varying the flora can bring about a burst of life and color, transforming the entire garden. Similarly, your minds thrive on novelty and challenge. When you venture into new territories, you stimulate your brain, break the cycle of monotony, and open yourself up to a world of possibilities.

Trying something different doesn't mean abandoning your primary goals or interests. Instead, it's about injecting diversity into your life, which can catalyze new ideas and approaches. Engaging in a new hobby, learning a new skill, or immersing yourself in an unfamiliar environment can reignite the passion and creativity that might have dulled over time. For instance, if you're a writer stuck in a creative rut, taking up painting or learning a musical instrument can stimulate different parts of your brain, potentially unlocking new avenues of inspiration for your writing.

The beauty of trying something new lies in the unknown. There's an inherent optimism and excitement that comes with exploring uncharted territory. This sense of discovery and the challenge of mastering something unfamiliar can be incredibly invigorating. It shifts your focus away from the pressures and expectations of your usual tasks, allowing your mind to relax and reset. This break can lead to moments of epiphany and a fresh outlook when you return to your original work.

Moreover, new activities can connect you with different people and communities, broadening your social circle and exposing you to diverse viewpoints. These interactions can further fuel your enthusiasm and provide insights you wouldn't encounter within your usual sphere. Sometimes, the best ideas and solutions come from the most unexpected places, and engaging with new people and experiences can be a treasure trove of inspiration.

There's also a psychological benefit to venturing into new activities. When you successfully navigate unfamiliar territory, it boosts your confidence and self-efficacy. The satisfaction of overcoming the initial challenges of a new endeavor can reinforce your belief in your abilities, spilling over into other areas of your life. This newfound confidence can make you more resilient and better equipped to handle setbacks in your primary pursuits.

> Humans are inherently adventurous beings. Your ancestors thrived because they explored, discovered, and adapted to new environments. This spirit of exploration is deeply embedded in your nature. Trying something completely different reconnects us with this primal urge to explore and discover, fulfilling a fundamental human need. When you embrace this adventurous side, you satisfy your curiosity and enhance your resilience and adaptability.

For instance, if you're an entrepreneur feeling bogged down by business challenges, taking a cooking class or joining a hiking club can provide a much-needed mental break. The joy of mastering a new recipe or reaching the peak of a mountain can reignite your sense of achievement and offer a fresh perspective on the problems you face in your business. The skills and patience you cultivate in these new activities can often translate into your primary work, offering innovative approaches and renewed determination.

Trying something completely different also combats the detrimental effects of burnout. When you're stuck in a repetitive cycle, it's easy to become mentally and emotionally exhausted.

Introducing variety into your routine can act as a mental refresh button, alleviating stress and rejuvenating your spirit. It's akin to taking a scenic detour during a long journey; it might seem like a diversion, but it can ultimately make the trip more enjoyable and sustainable.

These new experiences can also foster a more profound fulfillment and happiness. Engaging in diverse activities enriches your life, making it more balanced and well-rounded. It prevents your identity from becoming too narrowly defined by a single pursuit, allowing you to find joy and meaning in multiple areas. This multifaceted approach to life can make you more adaptable and open to change, invaluable qualities in both personal and professional realms.

Ultimately, stepping out of your comfort zone and trying something different is a powerful strategy to sustain momentum and reignite your passion. It's about embracing the journey of lifelong learning and discovery. Every new experience adds to your repertoire of skills and knowledge, making you more versatile and resilient. It's about understanding life is not a straight path but a rich tapestry of diverse experiences collectively enhancing your growth and fulfillment.

In the grand mosaic of life, each new activity and experience adds a unique tile. Embracing new challenges and diversifying your activities can transform how you approach your goals, infusing them with renewed energy and a fresh perspective. So, when you feel your momentum waning, remember sometimes the best way to move forward is to take a step in a completely different direction. Dive into the unknown with curiosity and enthusiasm, and you might find that the detour leads you exactly where you need to be.

GAIN PERSPECTIVE

*****

Losing momentum is an inevitable part of personal and professional growth. During these moments of stagnation, you often feel the weight of doubt and frustration. However, instead of succumbing to these feelings, you can take a proactive approach by becoming your coach. By analyzing and understanding the reasons behind your loss of momentum, you can develop a strategic plan to regain it, transforming setbacks into opportunities for growth.

Acting as your coach begins with a deep and honest self-assessment. This requires stepping back from the daily grind and reflecting on what's causing the slowdown. Are you overwhelmed by the sheer volume of tasks? Is there a specific challenge sapping your energy and enthusiasm? Or perhaps a lack of clear goals leads to a sense of aimlessness? Identifying the root cause is crucial. It's like diagnosing an illness; you can't treat it effectively without understanding what's wrong. By isolating the factors contributing to the loss of momentum, you lay the groundwork for a targeted and effective strategy.

Once the underlying issues are identified, the next step is to break them down into manageable parts. As your coach, you must dissect each problem and understand its components. For instance, if procrastination is a significant factor, explore why it's happening. Is it due to fear of failure, lack of interest, or poor time management? Each of these reasons requires a different approach. Understanding the specifics allows you to tailor your strategy to address each issue effectively.

After a thorough analysis, it's time to develop a plan of action. This plan should be realistic and attainable, focusing on gradual progress rather than immediate perfection. Start by setting clear, achievable goals. These goals act as milestones, giving you a sense of direction and purpose. For example, if you're struggling with time management, your first goal could be to create a daily schedule and stick to it. Small victories build confidence and momentum, paving the way for tackling more significant challenges.

In addition to setting goals, it's essential to establish a routine supporting sustained effort. This routine should include regular check-ins with yourself to monitor progress and adjust your strategy as needed. Consider it a coaching session where you review what's working, what isn't, and why. This iterative process ensures you stay on track and continue to make progress, even if it's incremental.

Another key aspect of acting as your coach is maintaining a positive and encouraging mindset. Coaches inspire and motivate their athletes; you must do the same for yourself. Celebrate your achievements, no matter how small, and use them as fuel to keep going. Acknowledge the effort you're putting in and remind yourself of the bigger picture. Self-compassion and positive reinforcement are crucial in sustaining momentum.

Additionally, sometimes, it's necessary to take a step back and allow yourself a moment of rest. Pushing through burnout is counterproductive and often leads to further loss of momentum. Recognize when you need a break and use this time to recharge. This is not a sign of weakness but a strategic move to maintain long-term productivity and well-being. Rest can provide clarity and rejuvenate your enthusiasm, making it easier to return to your goals with renewed vigor.

> Furthermore, being your coach means continuously seeking growth and improvement. This might involve learning new skills, seeking feedback from others, or exploring new perspectives. Staying curious and open to new ideas can keep you engaged and motivated. It's about creating a dynamic environment where you are constantly evolving and adapting, which naturally sustains momentum.

In conclusion, losing momentum is a natural part of any journey but doesn't have to be a permanent setback. By acting as your coach, you can analyze and understand the reasons behind the slowdown, develop a strategic plan to address them and foster a positive and encouraging environment for yourself. This proactive approach transforms challenges into opportunities, ensuring you regain momentum and build resilience and adaptability for the future. Embrace the role of being your coach, and sustaining momentum becomes a manageable and rewarding endeavor.

Integrate Regular Reflection and Adjustment Periods

Maintaining momentum involves more than a continuous push forward; it requires regular reflection and adjustment periods. These moments of introspection allow you to evaluate your progress, recognize achievements, and identify areas that need improvement. This approach helps sustain momentum and ensures your efforts are aligned with your long-term goals.

To implement this, set aside specific weekly or monthly times to thoroughly review your activities and progress. During these sessions, ask yourself critical questions: What have I accomplished? What challenges did I encounter? How did I overcome them, or why did they persist? This reflection helps you gain insights into your patterns of success and areas where you might be slipping.

Based on your reflections, make necessary adjustments to your strategies and goals. This might involve tweaking your daily routines, changing your approach to specific tasks, or setting new priorities. Regularly recalibrating your actions based on what you've learned ensures you remain agile and responsive to successes and setbacks. This ongoing process of reflection and adjustment keeps your efforts fresh and focused, sustaining your momentum.

Leverage the Power of Community and Accountability

Another powerful way to sustain momentum is by leveraging the power of community and accountability. Surrounding yourself with a supportive network can provide both motivation and practical assistance in your journey. Whether joining a professional group, finding a mentor, or participating in a peer support network, having others to share your goals and progress with can significantly enhance your ability to maintain momentum.

Accountability partners or groups can be particularly effective. These are individuals or teams with whom you regularly share your progress and setbacks. The mutual commitment to report on your activities creates a sense of responsibility and can drive you to stay consistent in your efforts. Knowing others are aware of your goals and are expecting updates can be a strong motivator to keep moving forward.

Moreover, engaging with a community can offer new perspectives and ideas you might not have considered. It allows for exchanging strategies and experiences, which can help you overcome obstacles and stay inspired. Seeing others in your community achieve their goals can reignite your enthusiasm and remind you of the possibilities.

By integrating regular reflection and adjustment periods and leveraging the power of community and accountability, you can create a dynamic and supportive environment that sustains your momentum and enriches your journey to your goals. These practices ensure you remain adaptable, motivated, and connected, making it easier to maintain a steady and productive course over the long term.

IMPLEMENT A CHALLENGE DAY.

*****

Complacency is often the unseen adversary lurking in the shadows. It's easy to fall into the comfort of routine, where the familiar rhythms of daily life lull us into a state of stagnation. Yet, buried beneath the safety net of familiarity lies a vast landscape of untapped potential and undiscovered talents waiting to be unearthed. This is where a "challenge day" emerges as a beacon of possibility—a day dedicated to pushing the boundaries of what you believe yourself capable of, venturing beyond the confines of your comfort zones, and embracing the exhilarating unknown.

Imagine waking up on a crisp Monday morning, the air charged with anticipation and excitement. Instead of the usual routine, today holds the promise of adventure, of embarking on a journey into uncharted territory.

> This is the essence of challenge day—a weekly ritual to inject a healthy dose of novelty and excitement into your lives. It's a day where the mundane is replaced by the extraordinary, where the familiar is cast aside in favor of the unfamiliar.

For some, the challenge day may take learning a new skill—a language or the art of playing a musical instrument. For others, it could involve tackling a project that has long been relegated to "someday," whether starting a blog, painting a masterpiece, or building a piece of furniture from scratch. The key is not necessarily in the outcome but in the process itself—stretching beyond your perceived limitations and embracing the discomfort of growth.

One of the most remarkable aspects of the challenge day is its ability to foster resilience and adaptability in adversity. Stepping outside your comfort zone inevitably invites discomfort and uncertainty, yet it is within these moments of pain that actual growth occurs. By exposing yourself to new experiences and unfamiliar situations, you cultivate the resilience to navigate life's inevitable twists and turns with grace and fortitude.

Moreover, the challenge day is a powerful antidote to the monotony and routine that can quickly dull the senses and dampen the spirit. In a world saturated with distractions and obligations, carving out dedicated time for exploration and experimentation becomes an act of rebellion—a declaration of autonomy and self-determination. It's a reminder your lives are not predetermined scripts but open-ended narratives waiting to be written.

Perhaps most importantly, the challenge day invites us to embrace the inherent joy of learning and discovery. In a society obsessed with productivity and achievement, we often forget the simple pleasure of engaging with the world with a sense of childlike wonder and curiosity. Whether we succeed or fail in our endeavors is ultimately secondary to the exhilarating experience of trying something new, daring to dream, and reaching for the stars.

So, as the sun sets on another challenging day, you are left with a profound sense of fulfillment and satisfaction, knowing you have dared to venture beyond the confines of your comfort zones and embrace the boundless possibilities that lie beyond. And as you drift off to sleep, you carry with us the indelible reminder that life is not meant to be lived on autopilot but savored with all the gusto and fervor of a grand adventure.

HARNESSING PHYSICAL MOTION

*****

This concept explores the relationship between physical movement and sustaining momentum as a novel approach to maintaining productivity and motivation.

The premise lies in the understanding movement begets momentum. Just as an object tends to stay in motion, individuals who engage in physical movement find themselves more inclined to sustain momentum in their endeavors. This concept emphasizes the interconnectedness between physical activity and mental agility, highlighting how movement catalyzes maintaining forward progress.

One practical application of this concept is the integration of short bursts of physical activity into daily routines. Whether it's a brisk walk around the block, a quick session of stretching and yoga, or even a spontaneous dance break, these moments of movement invigorate the body and stimulate the mind. By infusing periods of physical activity throughout the day, individuals can prevent stagnation and keep their energy levels high, thus sustaining momentum in their tasks and goals.

Furthermore, movement can also be used to overcome mental blocks and inertia. When faced with a challenging task or creative rut, taking a break to engage in physical activity can provide a much-needed mental reset. Whether going for a run, hitting the gym, or doing some jumping jacks, moving the body stimulates blood flow to the brain, increasing alertness and cognitive function. This renewed mental clarity can help individuals break through barriers and reignite their enthusiasm for their projects, thus sustaining momentum in the long run.

Another aspect of this concept involves leveraging the power of movement to foster collaboration and teamwork. Group activities such as team sports, group fitness classes, or even outdoor adventures like hiking or kayaking can promote camaraderie and teamwork among colleagues or friends. By participating in these shared experiences, individuals reap the physical benefits of movement, strengthen social bonds, and create a supportive network that encourages ongoing growth and momentum.

Additionally, incorporating movement into goal-setting and planning can enhance motivation and accountability. For example, setting specific milestones tied to physical achievements, such as completing a certain number of workouts or reaching a certain level of physical fitness, can provide tangible markers of progress and serve as powerful motivators to keep pushing forward. By intertwining physical movement with goal achievement, individuals can create a synergistic relationship that fuels sustained momentum and progress.

Overall, "Movement Momentum" emphasizes the connection between physical activity and mental well-being, highlighting how movement can catalyze momentum in various aspects of life. By prioritizing movement and integrating it into daily routines, individuals can unlock new levels of productivity, creativity, and motivation, ultimately leading to tremendous success and fulfillment in their endeavors.

CONCLUSION

The force of momentum is within your grasp, ready to propel you. The journey ahead is filled with possibilities, challenges, and opportunities.

Momentum is not just a concept; it's a force that drives you to your goals. It's the energy generated when you align your vision with relentless determination, creative thinking, and a commitment to excellence. The force of momentum is dynamic and can be harnessed in any area of your life.

The path to lasting success extends beyond this book. It's a lifelong pursuit filled with triumph, challenge, and growth moments. By applying the principles of momentum, adaptability, innovation, leadership, and resilience, you're equipped to navigate this journey with purpose and determination.

Your personalized momentum blueprint is the roadmap to your success. It's a dynamic guide that helps you set goals, formulate strategies, and take decisive actions. Your blueprint is a living document that evolves with you, allowing you to adapt to changing circumstances and seize new opportunities.

Excellence is not a destination; it's a continuous journey. Your commitment to excellence fuels your momentum and drives you to reach new heights. It's about setting high standards, embracing innovation, and persevering through challenges.

The world is filled with possibilities, waiting for those who dare to seize them. Your journey to lasting success is an exploration of these possibilities. Whether you're an athlete, a leader, an entrepreneur, or an individual seeking personal growth, momentum is your ally in this quest.

Remember that success is not a destination but a journey. Your commitment to embracing the warrior's spirit and innovative mindset will empower you to overcome challenges, seize opportunities, and achieve remarkable feats. The force of momentum is your constant companion, propelling you to lasting success in every aspect of your life.

Acknowledgments

*****

Stephanie Cunha would like to thank you for reading this book. I truly hope you can apply a concept from this work to help you in your athletic development and life. I want to thank all your contributors, collaborators, and clients at Mental Accelerator. You are grateful for the opportunity to serve you each day.

By Mental Accelerator

For more content on the athlete's mindset, visit us at:

www.MentalAccelerator.com

www.ingramcontent.com/pod-product-compliance
Lightning Source LLC
LaVergne TN
LVHW011420080426
835512LV00005B/173